BEYOND THE BALANCE SHEET:

Human Competencies in Banking of North East India

BEYOND THE BALANCE SHEET:

Human Competencies in Banking of North East India

Debanjalee Chakravorty
Jaynal Uddin Ahmed

KALPAZ

Published by

Kalpaz Publications
C-30, Satyawati Nagar,
Delhi – 110052
Ph.: 011-47034999, 9811692060
www.kalpazpublications.com
E-mail: kalpaz@hotmail.com

Distribution Network
gyanbooks.com
India, USA, Canada, UK, Australia, France

ISBN: 978-93-5722-528-1 (HB)
First Published, 2025

Printed at: Gyan Press, Delhi.

BEYOND THE BALANCE SHEET:
Human Competencies in Banking of North East India

Author: DEBANJALEE CHAKRAVORTY, JAYNAL UDDIN AHMED

Dedicated

To

KAMAKHYA PROSAD CHAKRABORTY

(whose wisdom, values, encouragement, and blessings have been a source of inspiration for our research)

Contents

Acknowledgment

The research work on this book titled"Beyond the Balance Sheet: Human Competencies in Banking of North East India"has been one of the most pleasing and certainly the most intellectually challenging jobs. Nevertheless, the work would not have been possible without the academic assistance and support of academicians and research scholars. At the very outset, we sincerely express our heartfelt gratitude to the Almighty, without whose blessings nothing can be done.

The academic motivation received from time to time from Prof. Rajive Mohan Pant, Vice-Chancellor, Assam University, Silchar; Prof. Chinmoy Roy, Tripura University, Agartala; Prof. G. D. Sharma, Vice-Chancellor, University of Science & Technology, Meghalaya; Prof. S. S. Khanka, Retd. Professor of National Institute of Financial Management, Faridabad; Prof. Abhigyan Bhattacharjee, North Eastern Hill University, Meghalaya; Prof. Kh. Devananda Singh, Nagaland University; Prof. Ranjit Singh, Indian Institute of Information Technology, Allahabad; Prof. Parag Shil, Prof. Dibyojyoti Bhattacharjee and Prof. Debomalaya Ghosh, Assam University, Silchar, are gratefully acknowledged.

We are deeply grateful to our colleagues and friends in academia for their collaboration and support in pursuing our academic interests. We also acknowledge the academic guidance and emotional support provided by our family members throughout this scholarly endeavor. In particular, we highly appreciate the steadfast support and encouragement offered by Mrs. Shipra Bhattacharjee and Mr. Prazzal Bhowmick.

We would like to acknowledge the contributions of bank employees of Private Sector Banks for assisting us with the fieldwork of this study and participating in it. Moreover, the work would have been incomplete without the contribution of the respondents to the surveys.

Finally, weare obliged to Mr. Amit Garg, Director, Gyan Books Pvt. Ltd, New Delhi, for accepting the manuscript and bringing out this volume in an elegant manner.

Debanjalee Chakravorty

Jaynal Uddin Ahmed

Preface

In the evolving landscape of management research, the study of human competencies has emerged as a cornerstone in understanding organizational effectiveness. Yet, while extensive research has been conducted on competency frameworks in metropolitan and industrial regions, the nuanced and underexplored geography of North-East India remains relatively marginalized in academic literature. This work seeks to bridge that gap.

Rooted in rigorous empirical investigation, this book examines ***Beyond the Balance Sheet: Human Competencies in Banking of North East India*** offering both theoretical and applied insights for scholars of Human Resource Management, Organizational Behavior, and Regional Studies. It systematically unpacks the interplay between individual capabilities and institutional demands within three prominent private banking institutions—Axis Bank, ICICI Bank, and HDFC Bank—operating in one of India's most geographically and culturally distinctive zones.

Drawing on established model such as the Iceberg Model, the study contextualizes these frameworks within the socio-economic realities of the North-Eastern states. It critically examines how core competencies—spanning knowledge, skills, attitudes, motives, and values—are manifested, assessed, and aligned with strategic organizational goals in a region characterized by infrastructural constraints, low financial penetration, and rich ethnic diversity.

Beyond its empirical contributions, the book presents a compelling rationale for expanding the lens of competency research beyond urban and industrial settings. It invites researchers to consider regional dynamics, contextual sensitivities, and the socio-cultural fabric that shape workforce capabilities and institutional outcomes in less mainstream yet equally vital sectors of the Indian economy.

This study stands as both a scholarly contribution and a foundational reference for future inquiry into regional competency mapping. It is intended to stimulate further academic discourse, inspire comparative research across geographies, and support policy formulation for capacity building in India's frontier regions.

The 14th May 2025 **Debanjalee Chakravorty**

Jaynal Uddin Ahmed

Introduction to the Book Edition

This book is an outcome of a doctoral journey that began with a simple yet pressing question: *Are the competencies of bank employees in North-East India adequately aligned with the demands of their roles and regional challenges?* From that central question emerged a complex research endeavor involving a blend of conceptual modeling, institutional analysis, and extensive fieldwork across multiple banking organizations.

Designed with academic readers and researchers in mind, the structure of this book mirrors the rigor expected in graduate and postgraduate scholarship. It begins with a comprehensive review of competency theories and models, followed by an in-depth analysis of the Iceberg Model's applicability in the regional banking context. The empirical chapters draw from rich primary data and statistical tools such as ANOVA and Relative Importance Index, offering measurable insights into knowledge, skills, self-concept, traits, and motivational competencies.

While the study is grounded in the banking sector, its implications are interdisciplinary. Scholars in economics, public policy, human resource development, and regional planning will find value in the book's broader narrative on talent deployment, workforce resilience, and regional capacity-building. Additionally, the focus on three leading private banks—Axis Bank, ICICI Bank, and HDFC Bank—provides institutional diversity, making the research applicable across different organizational scales.

This edition is meant to reach a wider scholarly audience. It is not only a dissertation but a resource—a call for continued research into the often-overlooked human resource ecosystems of North-East India. It is hoped that the findings and models presented herein will inform future academic inquiries, development policies, and HR strategies in comparable regional contexts.

Chapter - 1

Introductory

1.1 Introduction

Globalization and increased competitive pressures have made the role of managerial competencies more prominent in improving the organization's performance, efficiency, and competitive interest (Scarbrough, 2000). Nowadays, organizations are concerned about competence to gain competitive advantage. Commercial banks are required to prepare themselves in terms of skill sets which would make their organizations competitive. The individuals believe in excelling which will help them to improve their core competency. The 1990s of the 20th century saw the development of the notion of competency management. The aforementioned approach focused on the issue of matching employees' competencies to the specific requirements of the firm.. Haldar (2011) stated that "Winners do not do different things, they do things differently". Sound technical knowledge and skills are not only the basis of the distinctive competence of employees; different behaviors make them excellent, exceptional, and distinguished in their respective fields. Competencies provide a means for looking at those behaviors and differentiating the best from the rest. The business scenario in today's world is characterized by mergers, acquisitions, growing competition, threats, and uncertainties so managers face stressful situations. Therefore, the competency approach is the basis for a variety of initiatives and is adaptable and flexible. It customizes the execution of the training program and helps validate and evaluate the suitability considering the participant profile and training needs.

Business organizations are based on organizational development and its effectiveness. In the cutthroat competition that prevails in the business world, employee competency plays an important role if victory is to be rejoiced. An amalgamation of Knowledge, Skills, Attitudes (KSAs), Values, and Motives can be referred to as the competencies that are prevalent for an organization to sustain. Jain (2013) stated that Chanakya's Arthashrastha is considered the first book on competency which is still considered to be the finest book for management professionals and practitioners. Bharthvajan (2013) emphasizes that human resources deals with assigning the right people to the right job and this is attainable if the organization analyses the competencies that are present in the workplace in the form of human assets. The competency mapping analysis has been rigorously used by corporations from the tourism, medical, banking, and hospitality industries for the benefit of the employees in general and organizations at large. Various competency-based models have also been suggested by academicians and researchers for the performance appraisal of employees.

Competencies help in redirecting and articulating what the employees contribute to the organization. Competency mapping identifies the core competencies required for that organization and then uses them for various HR processes like Job Analysis, Job Evaluation, Training and Development, etc. Competencies vary from Job to Job, Department to Department, and so on. For different departments and different jobs, these competencies have separate weightage. Accordingly, Competency Mapping rates the employees' skills and assists them to improve their competence which is important for their career development (Jain, 2013).

Human resource management is a process of bringing people and organizations together so that the goals of each other are met. Nowadays, it is not possible to show a good financial or operating report unless personnel relations are in order. Over the years, highly skilled and knowledge-based jobs have increased while low-skilled jobs are decreasing (Yuvaraj, 2011). This calls for future skill mapping through proper HRM initiatives. Indian organizations are also witnessing a change in systems, management cultures, and philosophy due to the global alignment of Indian organizations. There is a need for multi-skill development. These kinds of skills can be determined when one is ready to do the work. Every well-managed firm should have well-defined roles and a list of competencies required to perform each role effectively. Therefore, competency mapping is one of the most accurate means of identifying the job and behavioral competencies of an individual in an organization (Sharma and Khanna, 2015).

Tejaswari et. al (2016) in the paper discuss the dynamism of Indian companies and the emerging competition in the global markets that have called for skill mapping for the employees which raises the need for competency mapping. Recruitment and selection have been a very important task for recruiters and the best-fitted person must be recruited for the right job. However, it is not always possible to identify the best from the rest. Therefore, organizations these days are more focused on competency development. Every task done by the managers in the organization requires competency in knowledge and skills appropriate to the task. Thus competency is a skill statement and not a task statement.

To gain an advantage in the competitive market, commercial banks need to reconsider how a customer thinks about a particular bank, and thus banks need to focus their competencies in the areas that extend beyond budgeting and saving. By gaining a true understanding of their customers' financial situation, banks can make themselves indispensable partners in their customers' personal and business lives.

With rapid changes taking place in the financial landscape, bankers have become more customer-centric, technology-savvy, highly qualified, flexible, and agile with behavioral skill sets that are more comprehensive in the present context. The quality of human capital will increasingly become the cutting periphery of competitiveness. Having competent staff to deliver high-quality products and services is important to build customer confidence and goodwill, driving customer satisfaction, enhancing reputation, and ultimately realizing an individual bank's corporate vision and strategic goals. Therefore, banking institutions particularly private banks are interested in ensuring competency and professionalism to serve their customers better. The winners in this sector will be the players who can understand the customer better, fulfill customer needs, and achieve a high level of customer retention. To understand the needs of the customers and fulfill them, the bank employees both at the managerial and clerical level must have the required level of competency in their behavioural skills. For this, they must aim to improve their skills as and when new changes occur (Nair, 2014). This has prompted us to undertake a study on competency mapping of bank employees, particularly private sector banks.

Human Resource Management these days is more dependent on personnel relations where more importance is given to knowledge and skill-based jobs and low skill-based jobs are eliminated, which in turn increases the demand for competency mapping at all levels in the organization. Skill mapping is also used as a procedure to identify the gray areas needed for betterment of performance. Competency mapping is also a way of identifying an employee's multi-skill development. (Yuvaraj,2011)

1.2 Operational Definitions of Related Concepts

From the above review of literature and theoretical understanding, the present research sets the following operational definitions.

1.2.1 ***Competency:*** Competencies are generic knowledge motives, traits, social roles or skills of a person linked to superior performance on the job. It is an underlying characteristic of an individual that is casually related to effective and/or superior performance.

1.2.2 ***Competency Map:*** A competency map is a list of an individual's competencies that represent the factors most critical to success in given jobs, departments, or industries that are part of the individual's current career plan.

1.2.3 ***Competency Profiling:*** It is the process of identifying the Knowledge, Skills, Attitude (KSAs), and judgment required for effective performance in a particular company/business-specific profession.

1.2.4 ***Competency Mapping:*** Competency mapping is not only finding the right people for the right job but also a process of identifying key competencies for a particular position in an organization, and then using it for job evaluation, recruitment, training and development, performance management, succession planning, etc. It is the process of identification of the competencies required to perform successfully in a given job or role or a set of tasks at a given point in time.

1.3 *Overview of Competency Map and Competency Mapping*

Garrett (2008) stated that a competency map is a list of an individual's competencies that represent the factors most critical to success in given jobs, departments, organizations, or industries that are part of the individual's current career plan. Competency mapping is a process of identification of the competencies required to perform successfully a given job role, or set of tasks, at a given point in time. The process consists of breaking down the job or role into its constituent elements or activities and identifying the competencies essentially required to perform the job successfully. All types of competencies, namely technical, managerial, behavioral/ interpersonal, conceptual, knowledge, attitudes, and skills are considered in competency mapping (Sanghi,2004). Nagaraju and Gowda (2009) highlighted that competency mapping is one such advanced practice that is widely being used by organizations today and it assesses the value of human capital and its development. In light of the above study, Hsieh, Lin, and Lee (2012) stressed that the current trends in human resource management place anxiety on the expansion and working of the term competency, particularly the important role it plays in improving job performance which in turn achieves heightened organizational competitiveness.

Competencies are a result of academic training and experience. Competency mapping can be beneficial for an individual who seeks to learn new things and be exposed to intellectually challenging work. Haldar (2011) stated that learning and development take place at three separate levels namely knowledge, skills, and competency. Sanghi (2004) elucidates the conceptual differences of these three. The paper refers to the fact knowledge comes through reading, skill develops through practicing and competence refers to applying skills needed for work. Kaur and Kumar(2013) mention in a paper that competency mapping establishes expectations for performance excellence, resulting in a systematic approach to professional development, improved job satisfaction, and better employee retention. Bharthvajan (2013) further stated that Competency Mapping juxtaposes two sets of data. One set is based on organizational workflow and processes.

It starts with a clear articulation of workflow and processes, including all quality and quantity requirements, inputs and outputs, decision criteria, and most importantly, internal and external customer requirements. For each step in each process, specific performance requirements are identified with all associated metrics and expectations. The other set of data is based on individual and group performance capabilities.

Solomon (2013) observed that large organizations may use some techniques to understand how to efficiently use each worker or how to combine the strengths of different employees to produce the highest quality work. Individuals may also find that this type of assessment can help them to prepare for a career change or advancement in a specific job field. Chaudhary and Singh (2016) examined emotional intelligence or emotional quotient (EQ) and the strengths of the individual in areas like team structure, leadership, and decision-making. It consists of breaking a given role or job into its constituent's task or activities and identifying the competencies (technical, managerial, behavioral, conceptual knowledge, attitudes, and skills) needed to perform the same successfully. Thus, competency mapping is the process of identification of the competencies required to perform successfully in a given job or role or a set of tasks at a given point in time.

1.4 Glimpse of Competency Mapping Models

Competency models provide tools for determining exactly what skills are required to meet the different needs of the present and the probable needs of the future. Competency models help to determine what behaviors the employees are required to perform and it could also ascertain the training needs of the people by identifying their skill gaps and deciding which of these gaps ought to be addressed immediately to ensure high performance (Sanghi, 2004). Over the years, various models have evolved, but almost all the models emerged from McClelland's method of determining what leads to superior performance.

1.4.1 *Lancaster Model of Competencies:*

Lancaster model of competencies was developed by Burgoyne

and Stuart (1976). This model has eleven competencies under three levels.

Level one:

Competence one: Command of basic facts awareness and knowledge about work and organization, key performance areas, and key result areas.

Competence two: Relevant professional knowledge, knowledge about management and business affairs.

Level two:

Competence one: Continuing sensitivity to events which includes information updating, and an open mind to all the events of business, organization, and people.

Competence two: Analytical, problem-solving, and decision-making skills.

Competence three: Social skills and abilities, like excellent communication both formal and informal, persuasion, peace-maker, resolving conflict, leadership, negotiation, and motivation.

Competence four: Emotional resilience

Competence five: Proactivity or inclination to respond purposefully to events.

Level three:

Competence one: Creativity, ability to come up with innovations and ideas, and an insight to choose the best one.

Competence two: Mental agility, alertness, and balanced mindset to respond quickly and accurately to problems.

Competence three: Balanced learning habits and skills.

Competence four: Self-knowledge

Figure: Lancaster Model of Competencies

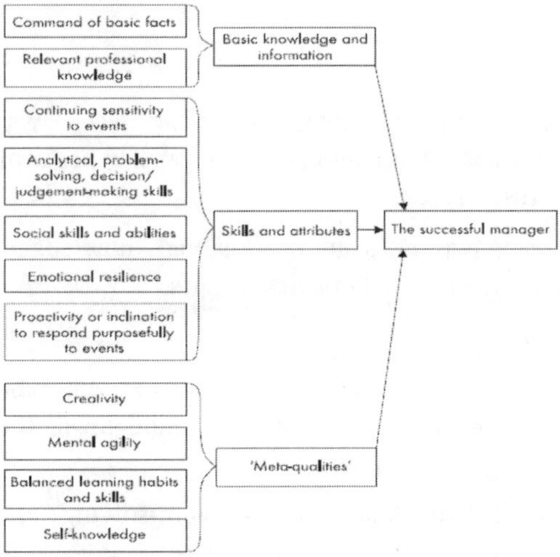

Source: Burgoyne, J.G. and Stuart, R. (1976)

1.4.2 *The Iceberg Model of Competency Mapping*

The origin of this model emerged from Sigmund Freud's 'Iceberg Model of Consciousness.' This model depicts the characteristics of competency. McClelland in the year 1973 developed the concept of competency. The various components of competencies can be represented at different levels of an iceberg. Managerial Competencies can be thought of as an iceberg, with skill and knowledge delineated at the top. In other words knowledge and skills are the visible or observable part of the competency. The other components of competencies being underlying elements are somewhat less visible but they have great influence and control over manifested or surface behaviour. Social roles, self-concept, traits, and motives are more hidden and deep-seated parts of personality. (McClelland, 1973).

Not all competencies are agreeable to training; they differ in the extent to which they can be taught. Domain knowledge and behavioral skills are most responsive to training interventions and training does display a positive impact on the characteristics. McClelland & Winter (1969) stated that changing motives and traits is possible, although the process is expensive. In reality, most organizations follow exactly the opposite; they recruit based on educational attributes viz. qualification, institute, etc., and presume that these candidates come with the desired traits and motives, and if that not being the case appropriate motives and traits can be drilled into them. Going by the above discussion, it can be inferred that from a cost-effectiveness standpoint, it makes sense to hire people with the appropriate motives and traits and train them in the knowledge and skills desired for a particular job or role.

The below surface components of competency in the Iceberg Model are the most complex and pose difficulty in measurement. Personality traits that are on the surface seem to be non-quantifiable. On deeper analysis, it is found to be measurable and open to evaluation when translated into behavioral terms.

Figure: Iceberg Model of Competency

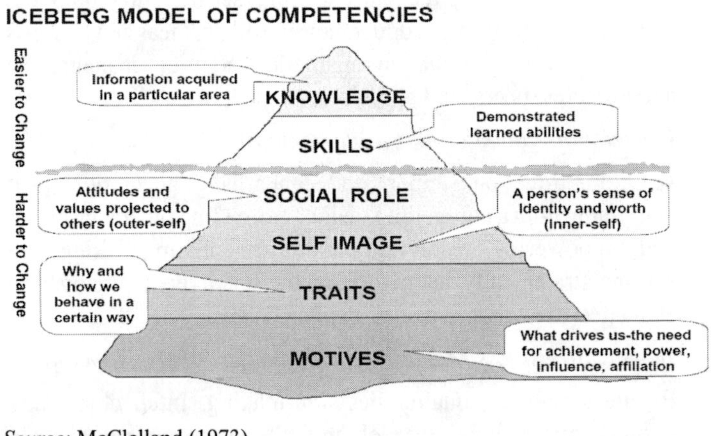

Source: McClelland (1973)

1.4.3 *Holistic Domain Model of Managerial Competencies*

The holistic Domain model expanded the form of the existing models of managerial competencies and incorporated key managerial competencies (Asumeng, 2014). The key elements in the proposed Holistic Domain Model of Managerial Competencies comprise six key domains: intrapersonal skills (Personal), interpersonal skills (Managerial, people domain), leadership skills, technical/business skills, career skills, and mentoring skills. In addition to the taxonomy competencies, protocols for measuring and assessing the sample competencies are provided. A summary of the model is presented in the table below:

Competency Sample Competencies/Behavioral Indicators Assessment

Intra-personal (Personal)

Emotional stability, self-control, core self-esteem, self-efficacy, self-awareness, courage, willingness to take a stand, career ambition, hardworking, achievement –orientation, perseverance, resilience, integrity, trustworthiness, patience, creativity, adaptability, self and other subordinates, colleagues and superiors.

Interpersonal (Managerial, people domain)

Building relationships, empathy communication skills, team building, networking, feedback seeking, sensitive to employees' concerns, listening to and understanding others ideas and interests, modest, warm/friendly, sympathetic, conflict management, subordinates, peers, and superiors.

Leadership (Managerial, people domain)

Providing direction, support, and standards for accomplishment, communicating a compelling vision, motivating others, inspiring, and empowering, resolving conflicts/negotiating, hiring, and staffing strategically, teamwork, managing diversity, innovation, evaluated by others, especially subordinates.

Technical/Business/Management (Managerial, task domain)

Business acumen, quality decision-making, intellectual capability, analytic thinking, problem-solving, functional/technical skills, planning, organizing ability, priority setting, performance-enhancing, managing human resources, managing information and material resources, innovation, administration, developing effective business strategy, delegating.

Self–evaluation, Evaluated by others-superiors, colleagues. -360-degree feedback/multi-system-multi-rater assessment.

Career (Personal)

Hardworking; goal achievement orientation, work capability/

efficacy, work commitment/perseverance, investing extra/ maximum inputs. Organizational support: political; socially astute, influential, interactive, socially networked. Objective: pay, upward progression/upward mobility, number of promotions, attainment of high occupational status, power and authority, prestigious jobs. Subjective/intrinsic, current job satisfaction, career satisfaction.

Objective- Evaluated by superiors, and colleagues. Subjective self-evaluation, 360 degrees feedback.

Mentoring (organizational citizenship behavior)

Personal- intrapersonal skills, interpersonal and communication skills, approachable, empathy, desire to help others, supportive, mentoring efficacy. Professional-career development skills, teaching/instructional, coaching, counseling, facilitating, supervisory, knowledge and experience of the mentee's area of work, knows organizational routines, procedures and policies, empowers the mentee, leadership skills, Personal- mentees/ subordinates, Professional-mentees, superiors, colleagues. -360 degrees feedback.

Figure: ***Holistic-Domain Model of Managerial Competencies***

Source: Asumeng (2014)

It is observed that almost all the aforesaid models suffer limitations one way or the other. The quantification of some variables theorized under some models (particularly in the Lancaster model and Holistic domain model) does not have any sense or least sense in the context of employees of private sector banks. Hence, an overview of the aforementioned models indicated that the Iceberg Model of competencies is relevant in a research work of this nature, particularly for understanding the competencies of private sector bank employees. Therefore, the Iceberg Model with minor modifications shall remain operational for the study.

1.5 Glimpse of the Private Sector Banks Taken Under Consideration

The literature derived will help us analyse the profile of the Banks compiled from the Annual Reports of the Banks. The banking and non-banking sectors faced major challenges of inflation, monetary policy tightening and geopolitical risks after Covid-19 pandemic. But the Indian Banking sector bounced back with improved asset quality and strong capital buffers. Despite the pandemic challenges, India is expected to remain the fastest growing major economy with estimated GDP growth rate of 6% in the financial year 2024. (Annual Reports, HDFC Bank, 2022-23)

Profile of the Sample Banks:

1.5.1 *Axis Bank Ltd.*

Axis Bank Ltd. is the fourth largest private sector bank in India. The bank offers the entire spectrum of financial services to customer segments covering large and mid-corporates, MSME, agriculture, and retail businesses. The integrated business lines include retail banking, with products and services occurred are loans, savings and retail term deposits, credit, debit and forex cards, bill payment services, wealth management, life insurance, government fund, mutual funds, etc. Wholesale and Commercial Banking caters to the needs of Corporates and MSME's with a strong emphasis on digital banking. The products offered are loans, current and corporate term deposits, payments, trade finance products, letters of credit, bank guarantees, foreign exchange, derivates, cash management services, commercial cards. The One Axis category provides products like investments, broking, asset management, and insurance, MSME digital insurance discounting platform, trustee services and payments.

The Bank offers distinctive financial solutions like expanding customer base, increased geographical reach and partnerships etc. The employee centric approach helps the bank gather the position of No 1 in employing people belonging to LGBTQIA + and persons with disability.

With a total of 65,500 banking outlets, 4910 branchesand 15,953 ATMs across the country (Annual Reports, 2022-23), an addition of 145 new branches in the year 2022-23 enabling the bank to reach out to a large cross-section of customers with an array of products and services. The bank also has nine overseas offices with branches in Singapore, Hong Kong, Dubai, Shanghai, and Colombo; representative offices in Dubai, Abu Dhabi, and Dhaka and an overseas subsidiary in London, UK (Jindal and Agarwal, 2016). Axis Bank is one of the first new-generation private sector banks to have begun operations in 1994. The bank was promoted in 1993, jointly by Specified Undertaking of Unit Trust of India (SUUTI), Life Insurance Corporation of India (LIC), General Insurance Corporation of India (GIC), National Insurance Company Ltd., The New India Assurance Company Ltd., The Oriental Insurance Company Ltd. and United India Insurance Company Ltd. The total number of employee base of the bank increased from 20624(2008-09) to 88726 as on 2022-23 (Annual Report, 2008-09, 2022-23Axis Bank Ltd.).

The bank's commitment to inclusive growth is catered with a total of 152 branches and 282 ATMs in North East India. In Nagaland, the second largest capture in network of branches is owned by Axis bank. (Axis Bank Press Release, August 23, 2022). The bank hired 18,792 bankers with 26% female representation in work force and 87 training hours per employee. (Annual Reports, 2022-23).

An overview of the financial profile highlights the deposits at Rs. 946945 crores, advances at Rs. 845303 crores, credit-deposit ratio at 89.26, profit after tax at 21933 crores, gross NPA at 2.02 %, net profit at Rs 21933 crores and profit per employee at 10.67 lacs.

Schedule V of the SEBI listing regulations, the board of directors have identified the following competencies to function effectively:

Accountancy, Agriculture, Banking, Co-operation, Information Technology, Infrastructure, Human Resources, Core industries, Economics, Finance, Small Scale Industry, Law, Payment and Settlement System, Risk Management and Business Management. (Annual Reports, 2022-23). Axis Bank stands 4th with market capitalization of 3.23 lac crores. (www.forbes.com)

1.5.2 *ICICI Bank Ltd*

ICICI Bank (Industrial Credit and Investment Corporation of India) is India's second largest private sector bank with total consolidated assets of Rs. 15,842.07 billion and profit after tax of Rs. 318.96 billion. (Annual Report, 2022-23, ICICI Bank Ltd). ICICI Bank currently has a network of 5900 Branches and 16,650 ATMs across India. ICICI Bank was originally promoted in 1994 by ICICI Limited, an Indian financial institution, and was its wholly-owned subsidiary. The principal objective was to create a development financial institution for providing medium-term and long-term project financing to Indian businesses. In the 1990s, ICICI transformed its business from a development financial institution offering only project finance to a diversified financial services group offering a wide variety of products and services, both directly and through several subsidiaries and affiliates like ICICI Bank.

The financial profile highlights the deposits at Rs. 11808.41billion, advances at Rs. 10196.38 billion, credit-deposit ratio at 86.34, profit after tax at Rs 318.96 billion, gross NPA at Rs 311.84 billion, net profit at Rs 318.96 billion and profit per employee at Rs 2.8 lacs. The bank has 124 branches operating in North-East India. (www.prokerala.com)

The bank puts an enormous focus on frontline employees as an initiative towards human capital to cater to a 360-degree customer engagement policy. Women comprise 32% of total employees and the average person learning days of 12.2 days in fiscal 2023. The focus was also on the industry-academia interface to create a bunch of skilled bankers. The human capital of the bank is guided by "One Bank, One Team, One ROE'. The employee-centric approach enables cross-functional collaboration, job rotation, skill training and capacity building, employee engagement, etc.

The bank follows the approach of customer 360° which means it offers a holistic banking experience. The approach is to take the entire bank to the customer and provide banking solutions as per their demand. ICICI Stack is one of the digital initiatives launched after the Covid-19 pandemic that provides uninterrupted solutions to customers in digital platforms.

The banks offer diversified business lines in Retail, Rural and Inclusive Banking, Small and Medium Enterprises and Business Banking, Wholesale Banking, International Business, Government Banking, etc. Periodic training sessions and information mailers are considered to be a part of knowledge enhancement programs. Employee retention and attracting a Liverpool of talented manpower is considered to be essential for strategic banking and cutthroat competition. Upskilling is thus considered to be of prime importance.

The skill domains of ICICI Bank consist of Cloud Computing, Automation, API and Micro services, Cyber Security, Data Engineering, Data Analytics, Project Management, Data Visualisation, etc. Skill mapping in Data Sciences, Design thinking, and Artificial intelligence is given to the employees. Over 12 million learning hours are invested in its employees and the average learning per day was around 12.2 days according to reports of Fiscal 2023. ICICI Bank stands 2nd in terms of market capitalization with a net worth of 7.07 lac crores. (www.forbesindia.com)

1.5.3 *HDFC Bank Limited*

HDFC Bank is India's largest private sector lender by assets. It is the leading private bank in India by market capitalization of 10.94 lac crores. (www.forbesindia.com) HDFC Bank was incorporated, with its registered office in Mumbai, India. HDFC Bank was founded in the year 1994 with permission from Reserve Bank of India after liberalization of Indian Banking industry.

The bank's distribution network has 47821 branches and 19727 ATMs. The equity shares of HDFC Bank are listed on the Bombay Stock Exchange and the National Stock Exchange of India. HDFC Bank caters to a wide range of banking services covering commercial and investment banking on the wholesale side and transactional / branch banking on the retail side. The bank has three key business segments viz, wholesale Banking, treasury, and **retail banking.** (Annual Report, 2022-23, HDFC Bank Ltd.). The bank is world's fifth largest bank by market capitalization as of August 2023. It is also the 16th largest employer in India with an employee strength of 173222 employees amongst which 95% are women hires as on 2022-23.

The financial profile highlights the deposits at Rs. 1883395 crores, advances at Rs. 1600586 crores, credit-deposit ratio at 84.98, profit after tax at Rs 44109 crores, gross NPA at Rs 1.12%, net profit at Rs 44109 crore and the volume of business per employee stands at 10.87 crore. The bank had 136 branches operating in North-East India as on November 13, 2019 and to be expanded to 200 branches in next few years. (Singh, 2019).

The bank focused on building the right competencies in terms of development factories and people capabilities. Initiatives such as Artificial Intelligence enablement, instituting innovation lab to create rapid prototypes, investment in low code platforms to enable automation at scale. Operational efficiencies are also monitored though cloud technologies. Diverse customer base, healthy channel mix, sourcing across geographies have been the key strategies of HDFC Bank. Regular interaction, cross sell and management of attrition have been the leading competencies. The banks spends an average of 18.02 hours on training of employees. The bank focuses on employee engagement, culture and employee experience, employee wellness and safety, learning and development, etc. The training also focuses on product knowledge, sales technique, communication, compliance and customer relationship management because after pandemic, there has been a shift to digital and contactless banking.

The multi-dimensional performance measurement system aligns organizational goals with key objectives. Employees make a self-evaluation of their performance based on their roles and responsibilities. Then discussions are conducted by the Appraiser and the Appraise jointly which includes feedback on performance, competencies, development needs and career aspirations. This system of performance appraisal gives scope for career progression, development of knowledge and skills according to one's potential and interest. The digital transformation of the bank is achieved by building competencies of the employees. 'Trallbase' is a program initiated for the employees that focuses on key competencies and management essentials to polish their effectiveness. 'Leadership Competency Framework' and 'Functional Capability Framework' are the guidelines for identifying and developing key competencies.

1.6 Rationale for North East India's Banking Competency Assessment

Banks helps to encourage inclusive growth and lessen the vulnerable status of the impoverished and marginalized (Chakrabarty, 2009). On the other hand, China and India account for the second largest population without access to formal financial services, with over 190 million individuals not having bank accounts (Demirguc-Kunt et al., 2017). Additionally, Maity (2019) discovered that NER has a relatively lower level of financial inclusion than the national average.Bhandari(2018) inthe study aims to analyze the situation of banking infrastructure in the underdeveloped region of North-East India and its impact on overall socio-economic development. The study aims to determine the relationship between the underdeveloped banking infrastructure in the North-East region of India and its impact on the overall socio-economic development of the region. The study provides insights into the importance of having well-developed money markets and capital markets in order to effectively implement monetary policies and drive economic growth. Additionally, the study highlights the role of banks and financial institutions as key drivers of capital resources in the economy. By examining the banking infrastructure in the underdeveloped region of North-East India, this study seeks to shed light on the correlation between the state of financial development and overall socio-economic progress in the region.. In summary, the study aims to analyze the impact of underdeveloped banking infrastructure on the overall socio-economic development of North-East India.

In their study, Sahoo & Khundrakpam (2006) examined the sustained growth of banking indicators in the North-Eastern regionof India following the nationalization of major banks in 1969 and 1980, but found a retarding trend in banking parameters since the beginning of the 1990s.The study by Sahoo & Khundrakpam (2006) highlights the challenges faced by scheduled commercial banks in the North-Eastern regionof India and provides suggestions to enhance their financial intermediary role in the region. The study sheds light on the sustained growth of banking indicators in the North-Eastern region of India following the nationalization of major banks, but also emphasizes the decline in banking parameters since the 1990s. The study highlights the retarding trend in banking parameters since the beginning of the 1990s, suggesting potential impediments and providing suggestions for improving the financial intermediary role of scheduled commercial banks in the region.

In order to overcome these obstacles and promote banking and financial development in rural areas, it is crucial to address the topographical challenges, improve infrastructure, enhance entrepreneurship skills, strengthen law and order, shift towards a loan-based development strategy, expand the network of branches, develop customized financial products, improve loan recovery mechanisms, raise awareness about banking services, and upgrade payment systems. (Bhandari, 2018)

According to Thangasamy's (2014) observations, one of the ongoing complex issues for financial inclusion is North-Eastern India. The primary causes are: challenging topography, reduced population density, subpar infrastructure, insufficient communication capabilities, and issues with law and order. 3,250 settlements in the Northeastern Region had a population of more than 2,000 people in 2011 but no banking facilities. As of the end of September 2011, 1,031 communities were connected to financial channels.

According to Boro's (2015) report, there is a great possibility for financial institutions to consider alternatives to traditional brick and mortar branch banking due to the growing number of mobile users and internet penetration in both rural and urban areas. Due to political, physical, cultural, and socioeconomic divides, the eight states that make up North-East India have been ignored and cut off from the rest of main land India. This makes the region a valuable research area. The aim of his paper was to expand the research on technical innovation in the banking sector of Northeast India.

Bhandari (2018) opined that when compared to the national picture, the Northeast Region and its member states appear to be in relatively poor condition with regard to the banking development scenario. The underdevelopment of the banking position may be caused by the area's hilly topography, the presence of several tribes whose members are less aware of the benefits of banking services, the general lack of awareness among the populace, and the general lack of significance placed on the sector by those in charge of making policy. It's been suggested that the lack of large enterprises and other worthwhile initiatives in the area contributes to the poor banking and financial infrastructure in the area. In fact, it might be the other way around as well—that is, the absence of financial infrastructure is the reason why large projects and industries are not yet created.

The states of North East India differ from the rest of the nation in terms of geography, ethnicity, and culture. Even though the government has made great efforts to include the nations financially excluded, the northeastern region faces particular challenges because of its unique features, which make it challenging to replicate or implement the inclusion models that have been adopted nationwide. As a matter of fact, the growth of banks in Northeast India was a phenomena that emerged only after nationalization. Arunachal Pradesh and Mizoram did not have any commercial bank branches prior to the nationalization of banks in 1969. In Manipur and Nagaland, there were just two commercial bank branches that catered to the whole state. However, Assam was traditionally better served by banks than any other state in the region due to its oil and tea industries. Significant advancements in the banking sector have been accomplished in terms of both geographic and demographic expansion since then. Mizoram did not have any commercial bank branches prior to the nationalization of banks in 1969. In Manipur and Nagaland, there were just two commercial bank branches that catered to the whole state. nationalization of banks in 1969. Despite a modest beginning, the commercial banks' branch network in the area greatly grew. Still, India's banking development in North East India is still far behind that of any other state. (Chakma, 2014).

Inorder to satisfy the demands of the local people, it is imperative to evaluate the bankers' skills within the framework of the literature that has been referred. The competencies will assist in recognizing, gaining access to, and improving oneself in order to meet the demands of the places that are geographically isolated. The research will identify the employees' strongest competencies as well as any areas of grayness that require attention.

1.7 Need of the Study

The competency mapping is required to reinforce corporate strategy, culture, and vision. Competency Mapping establishes expectations for performance excellence, resulting in a systematic approach to professional development, improved job satisfaction, and better employee retention (Kaur and Kumar, 2013).

Selznick (1957) in his book '*Leadership in Administration*' said that the art of good management is the ability to make a practical assessment of an organization's suitability to its task or strategy. Competency mapping identifies an individual's strengths and weaknesses to help them to better understand themselves and to show them where career development efforts need to be directed (Shree et al, 2016). The banking sector has undergone a paradigm shift over the last few decades. Banks are now far off performing the conventional stereotypical activities of accepting deposits and extending loans but rather are seen as a vibrant sector with added responsibilities dedicated to ensuring and promoting the financial well-being of the customers. The banks are known as trustees of financial security for the people of a place. The change in the dynamics of the sector has not only made the performance of the sector to be significant for society but has also demanded the refinement and inculcation of additional skills amongst the employees of the sector. Human resources are considered as a source of competitive advantage for the banking sector. History of the sector and literature review has witnessed one of the biggest revolts in the sector when computerization was introduced in the 1980's substituting the manual performance of the employees. The resistance to such a change was triggered by the apprehensions of the employees about not being able to meet the standard. The bank employees feared the loss of their jobs. But with the graduation of time, the skills and the competencies of the employees were escalated to the level with the necessary training. The decade saw a path-breaking shift in the *modus operandi* of the sector. Since then the sector has seen a deluge of shifts either in the light of conforming to the macro-economic condition of the country or to gain a competitive edge in the industry. The unprecedented advancement in the sector particularly private banks has been mounted upon the roles human resources performs. The banks are now found to be more customer-centric and the employees are found to be more responsive. In addition to that, the employees of the modern times in the banks are expected to possess additional skills in the repertoire. The criticalities of the sector have not only been imposed upon the front-line employees to refine their skills but have introduced challenges for all the internal members of the sector irrespective of their hierarchy in the institutional structure. In light of all the issues, the fit of the employee's skills and abilities to the actual roles that they perform in the banks has been of paramount importance. An erroneous alignment of the competencies of the employees and the roles that they perform can bring misfortunes for the bank. The mapping of competencies is also equivalent to retaining the job morale of the employees as misfits can lead to an inability to perform to the level of expectation. All the factors have contributed to the need felt by the researcher to probe the matter and gain more insights into it. The research is intended to unfold the extent to which such fits are being maintained in the private banks operating in North-East India. The research claims to be of value for not only the administration of the banks but also indirectly for the customers of the banks. The administration can use the research to confirm whether the assignment of roles to the employees in the banks has been according to the competencies of the employees. Apart from the contribution of the research in suggesting the top management, the research can also contribute to validating whether the roles that the employees perform in the banks fit the skill sets of the employees. Such validation can evoke a sense of trust amongst the customers of the banks in the employees. The idea of the research stems primarily from its social contribution to unveiling the performance of the bank according to the roles assigned to the employees.

1.8 Research Problem

The banking industry has moved from a transaction-centric to a relationship-centric business approach. The actual change in the work dynamics now demands the performance of the employees in the banking sector to be more accountable. Banking is a knowledge-intensive, skills-based, and relationship-rich industry. In a progressive, complex, and more liberalized environment, the competitiveness of banks will depend significantly on the quality of human resources and the extent to which the industry can enhance these talents. The skill set of the employees in the banking sector now has become a major competitive weapon to cope with the ever-changing work environment in this sector. The selection process of employees in the banking sector has now become more rigorous. The sector is looked at and trusted upon whenever a society faces an economic crisis. Economists view the banking sector as a major tool for the implementation of their macroeconomic ideas set forth for either the rescue or the economic growth of a country. The sector has imperatively increased its service line to meet the growing needs of the customers. The dual work pressure on the sector to meet the ever-increasing demands of the customers and performing the role of custodians for the economic well-being of society has rendered the jobs of the employees very stressful. The demand of different stakeholders that is in such a varying form has imposed pressure even on the administration of the bank to assess the performance of the employees. The skill sets of the employees are supposed to be directed toward meeting the aforesaid expectations of the stakeholders. The private banks have been witnessing immense progress in the banking scenario. They are at the forefront of Internet Banking, Mobile Banking, ATMs, etc. Post liberalisation era has brought some significant changes in the banking scenario of India, where public sector and private sector banks are neck to neck with each other. The volatility of the foreign markets, the increasing number of NPAs, and frequent technological changes have made the need for competency mapping more significant (Rathod, 2015). The attrition rate has increased over the years in the case of private banks as witnessed by various studies (eg., Branham, 2005; Gelani, 2015; Diwedi, 2017). Hence, the bank has to adopt creative Human Resource Management strategies to counter attrition. In the case of public sector banks, the matter of job security is always higher than that of private banks. The career growth opportunities of the employees of private banks generally depend upon performance and competency, not on the level of seniority like public sector banks (Diwedi, 2017).

1.9 Display of the Book

1. Chapter-1: Introduction
2. Chapter-2: Review of Literature
3. Chapter-3: Research Methodology and Objectives
4. Chapter-4: Analysis and Interpretation
5. Chapter-5: Finding & Recommendations

References

Asumeng, M.A. (2014). Managerial Competency Models: A critical review and proposed holistic–domain model, *Journal of Management Research, Las Vegas, Nev: Macrothink Institute*, *6*(4), 1-20.

Axis Bank Press Release, August 23, 2022.https://www.axisbank.com/about-us/press-releases/axis-bank-dedicates-four-new-branches-in-the-north-east-in-the-presence-of-hon-finance-minister-of-india-nirmala-sitharaman

Axis Bank(2023). Annual Reports, Axis Bank. https://www.axisbank.com/docs/default-source/annual-reports/for-axis-bank/annual-report-for-the-year-2022-2023.pdf

Bhandari, G.S. (2018). A Study on the Banking Sector Scenario of the North-East Region of India. Anveshak, International Journal of Management, *7*(1), 9-22.

Bharthvajan, R. (2013).Competency mapping. *International Journal of Innovative Research in Science, Engineering and Technology, 2*(11),6288-6294.

Boro, K. (2015), "Prospects and challenges of technological innovationin banking industry of North East India", *Journal of Internet Banking and Commerce*, October

Branham, L. (2005). *The 7 Hidden Reasons Employees Leave*. Pensylvannia: Soundview Executive Book Summaries.

Burgoyne, J.G. and Stuart, R. (1976). The nature, use and acquisition of managerial skills and other attributes. *Personal Review, 5*(4), 19-20

Chakma, J. K. (2014), "Financial inclusion in India: A brief focus on Northeast India", *International Journal of Application or Innovation in Engineering & Management*, *3*(11)

Chakrabarty, K.C. (2009), "Banking: key driver for inclusive growth", *RBI Monthly Bulletin, 9*

Choudhary, S and Singh, S.(2010). A Study of Competency Mapping of Employees in Banking SectorWith Special Reference To ICICI Bank. *International Journal of Human Resources Management, 5*(3), 11-20

Demirguc-Kunt, A. and Klapper, L. (2013), "Measuring financial inclusion: explaining variation in use of financial services across and within countries", *Brookings Papers on Economic Activity, 1*

Dwivedi, G. (2017). A Study Of Increasing Employee Attrition Rate Of Axis Bank: Jhalawar (Rajasthan) Region. *International Journal of Science Technology and Management,6*(1), 732-745

Garrett, S.(2008).*Competency Mapping: What Is It and How It Can Be Done by Individuals*. Career Trainer.

Gelani, T.C. (2015). Comprehensive Study Of Attrition Strategy Of HDFC BANK in Ahmadabad Region. *RHIMRJ, 2*(5), 1-6.

Halder, K.U. (Ed.). (2011). *Human Resource Development* (3rd ed.). Oxford Higher Education.

Halder, K.U. (Ed.). (2011). *Human Resource Development* (3rd ed.). Oxford Higher Education.

HDFC Bank (2023). Annual Reports, HDFC Bank. https://www.hdfcbank.com/content/bbp/repositories/723fb80a-2dde-42a3-9793-7ae1be57c87f/?path=/Footer/About%20Us/Investor%20Relation/annual%20reports/pdf/Integrated%20Annual%20Report%202022-23.pdf

Hsieh, S.C., Lin, J.S. and Lee, H.C. (2012). Analysis on Literature Review of Competency. *International Review of Business and Economics,* 2, 25-50.

https://www.forbesindia.com/article/explainers/top-10-banks-india-by-market-cap/87913/1

ICICI Bank (2023). Annual Reports, ICICI Bank. https://www.icicibank.com/ms/aboutus/annual-reports/2022-23/icici/index.html

Jain, V.K. (2013).Competency Mapping in Indian Industries - A Case Study. *International Journal of Emerging Research in Management &Technology, 2*(10), 9-21

Jindal, M. and Agarwal, M. (2016). A Case Study of Axis Bank: Relationship between Empowerment and Job Satisfaction. *IJRSI, 3*(5), 122-126.

Kaur, J. and Kumar, V.(2013).Competency Mapping: A Gap Analysis. *International Journal of Education and Research,1*(1),1-9.

Kaur, J. and Kumar, V. (2013). Competency Mapping: A Gap Analysis. *International Journal of Education and Research, 1*(1), 1-9.

Maity, S. (2019), "Financial inclusion status in North Eastern region: an evidence of commercial banks", *International Journal of Research in Applied Management, Science and Technology, 4*(3)

McClelland, D. C. and Winter, D. G. (1969). *Motivating economic achievement.* Free Press.

McClelland, D.C. (1973). Testing for competence rather than for intelligence. *American Psychologist, 28*(1), 1–14.

Nagaraju, Y and Gowda, V.S. (2012). A Study of employee competency mapping strategies at select organization of Bangalore. *International Journal of Research in commerce and management, 3*(10), 176-182.

Nair, V.V. (2014). *Behavioural Competency Management with Special Reference To Commercial Banks Headquartered In Kerala* (Doctoral Dissertation, Cochin University of Science and Technology, Kerala, India

Rathod, T.R. (2015). *Employees competency mapping in private sector banks a study with special reference to private sector banks in hyderabad karnataka region*, (Doctoral dissertation, Gulbarga University, Karnataka)

Sahoo, A., & Kundrakapam, J. K. (2006), "A review of trends in banking indicators in North Eastern Region of India", *Reserve Bank of India Occasional Papers*, *27*(3).

Sanghi, S. (2004). *The Handbook of Competency Mapping Understanding, Designing, and Implementing Competency Models in Organizations*. Sage Publications Inc.

Sanghi, S.(2004). The Handbook of Competency Mapping Understanding, Designing, and Implementing Competency Models in Organizations, *Sage Publications Inc.*

Scarbrough, H. (2000). Recipe for Success. *People Management*, *9*(2), 32-5

Selznick, P. (1957). *Leadership in Administration: A Sociological Interpretation*. University of Calfornia.

Sharma, N. and Khanna, K. (2015). Competency Mapping. *Paripex-Indian Journal of Research, 4*(1), 161-163.

Shree, B, A. *et al.* (2016). A Study on Competency Mapping in Automobile Industry, *International Journal of Engineering Science and Computing, 6*(7), 8649-8657.

Shree, B, A. *et al.*(2016). A Study on Competency Mapping in Automobile Industry, *International Journal of Engineering Science and Computing, 6*(7), 8649-8657

Solomon, D,M. (2013). Competency Mapping – A Holistic Approach for Industries. *PARIPEX - Indian Journal of Research*, *2*(3).

Tejaswari, A. and Ambuli, T.V. (2016). A Study on Competency Mapping of Employees with reference to Murugappan and Company. *International Journal of Research Science and Management*, *3*(8), 21-31. https://ijrsm.com/index.php/journal-ijrsm/article/view/567

Thangasamy, E. (2014), Financial inclusion in North-East India: An analytical study, *International Journal of Commerce, Business and Management*, *3*(1)

Yuvaraj, R. (2011). Competency Mapping- A Drive for Indian Industries. *International Journal of Scientific and Engineering Research*, (8), 1-7.

Chapter -2

Review of Literature

2.1 Introduction

There exist a number of studies dealing with competency and competency mapping in India as well as global context. A thematic review of related literature has been presented in the following paragraphs to highlight the gap of the proposed study.

2.2 Theoretical Underpinning of Competency

The term Competency was initially coined by Richard E. Boyatzis (1982). The concept of human competence reached the forefront of human resource development with the concurrent work of the psychologists Robert White and David C. McClelland. White (1959) identified human trait as competence. McClelland (1973) originated an approach for predicting competence that was notably different from widely accepted intelligence tests of the time. He suggested that although intelligence influences performance, personal characteristics such as an individual's motivation and self-image, differentiate successful from unsuccessful performance and can be noted in a number of life roles that include job roles. McClelland (1973) opened up competency movement and demonstrates the data to show that traditional achievement and intelligence scores may not be able to predict job success and it is only the exact competencies required to perform a given job effectively and measuring them using a variety of tests, one can be sure about his profile.Hayes (1979) defines "competencies are generic knowledge motive, trait, social role or a skill of a person linked to superior performance on the job."Klemp (1980) stated that the Competency is 'an underlying characteristic of an individual which is casually related to effective and/or superior performance'. It is the ability to perform activities to the standards required in employment, using an approximate mix of knowledge, skill and attitude. The underlying principle of competency mapping is not just finding the right people for the right job. It is a process of identifying key competences for a particular position in an organisation, and then using it for job-evaluation, recruitment, training and development, performance management, succession planning, etc.

According to Boyatzis (1982), Competency is "an underlying characteristic of a person in that it may be a motive, trait or skill aspect of one's self – image or social role or body of knowledge". Spencer and Spencer (1993) in a study identified five types of competency characteristics consisting of motives, traits, self-concept, knowledge and skills. Motives are the psychological features that an individual consistently thinks about or wants that stimulate action. The traits are physical characteristics and consistent responses to situations or information. The self-concept is an individual's attitudes, values or self-image. Knowledge is the information that an individual has in specific content areas. The skill is the ability to perform a certain physical or mental task. Knowledge and skill competencies tend to be visible and relatively surface characteristics, whereas self-concept, traits and motive competencies are more hidden, deeper and central to personality. Surface knowledge and skill competencies are relatively easy to develop and training is the cost-effective way to secure the employee abilities. Expectations form opinions with respect to the likely performance of a product or service.

Parry (1996) defines competency as a cluster of related knowledge, skills and attitudes that affects a major part of one's job that are correlated with performance on the job or that can be measured against well accepted standards and that can be improved via training and development. UNIDO (2002) defines competency is a set of skills, related knowledge and attributes that allow an individual to successfully perform a task or an activity within a specific function or job. Garrett (2008) stated "competencies include the collection of success factors necessary for achieving important results in a specific job or work role in a particular organisation. Success factors are combinations of knowledge, skills and attributes (more historically called KSAs) that are described in terms of specific behaviours and are demonstrated by superior performers in those jobs or work roles. Attributes include personal characteristics, traits, motives, values or ways of thinking that impact an individual's behaviour."Currie and Darby(1995)stated that employees need to work in a multi-faceted work environment and therefore have to focus on enriching the competencies to meet the diversified work culture.

Boyatzis (2009) in the paper stated that competencies are a set of related but different sets of behavior organized around an underlying construct called the 'intent'. The behaviors are alternate manifestations of the intent, as appropriate in various situations and times.. Uddin et. al. (2012) is of the view that Competency mapping can also be used for coaching and succession planning, considering the significance of Competency Mapping for individual and organizational growth, the present study was undertaken. Efforts have been made to elaborate the various competencies with minute parameters and to correlate them with the managerial competence level.

The phrase Competence and Competency even though used interchangeably are not one and the same. Competence is a universal term relating to a person's typical ability and competencies are made up of the attributes of knowledge, skills and attitudes (Worlikar and Aggrawal, 2017). Bucker and Poutsma (2010) identifies competency as skills, knowledge, abilities and behavioural repertoires for successful completion of a task. The two words 'competence' and 'competency' are used alternatively but (Haldar, 2011) distinguishes the two words that are involved in performance management. Competence is about the ability to perform a job and describes what has to be done to perform a job. It is about the Intelligence Quotient. Competency describes how people behave in order to get a job done effectively and it is about the Emotional Quotient.

From the above definition of competencies, it can be said that competencies include the collection of success factors necessary for achieving important results in a specific job or work role in a particular organization. Success factors are combinations of knowledge, skills, and attributes (more historically called 'KSAs') that in those jobs or work roles and attributes include: personal characteristics, traits, motives, values or ways of thinking that impact an individual's behaviour.

An inventory of all competencies make it easier for the organizations to group the competencies together based on various aspects such as behavioural or soft competencies, managerial competencies, technical competencies, competencies for individual excellence, interpersonal relationships, etc. A manager is expected to have set of competencies categorized into organizational, role oriented, people centered, etc. Further these competencies are rated according to the skills and proficiencies of the employees. Some organizations may rate it as oh-oh, so-so, good and great while others may rate as baseline, collaborative productivity, ownership, managing complexity and expert and few others may rate it as level 1, 2, 3 and 4. The entire process of rating and labelling the competencies is termed as "competency matrix". (Tejaswari and Ambuli, 2016)

2.3 Need and Implications of Competency Mapping

Rainsbury et al(2002) suggested that there is an insufficient importance placed on the development of soft skills by many higher education institutions which teach employability skills in particular. Bath et al.(2004) opines that competencies should not be taught as a form of a check list but be integrated and contextualized into a curriculum. Hind et al.(2007) viewed that employability skills need to be embedded not only in any one module but must be shaped throughout the curriculum at all levels. Boyatzis (2007) identified that there were 19 generic competencies that outstanding managers tend to have and clubbed those 19 competencies into five distinct clusters such as goal and action management, leadership, human resources management, directing subordinates and focus on others. Yuvaraj (2011) has explained the job competencies that are required in manufacturing industry and gap analysis was also made to a limited extend. Uddin et. al. (2012) has explained various tools for implementing competency model including job analysis, job description, job specification, competency matrix, 360 degree feedback etc. The study suggested that competency mapping can also be used for coaching and succession planning. Tiwari (Mishra) (2012) generates a link between competency requirements and business management in India. Therefore new competencies related to employability have been identified which includes grasping of global systems, global issues, international dynamics, analytical skills, interpersonal skills, intellectual skills, multidisciplinary skills, inter-disciplinary skills, customer service, technical skills, critical management, passion , co-operation, team work, decision making, problem solving, motivation and initiative.

Atkinson(2015) in the paper summarized skills into four domain, cognitive domain referring to the intellectual skills or the application of knowledge, affective domain referring to the individual behaviour or the values and perceptions that an employee may possess, psychomotor domain referring to the intricate physical skills like usage of tools and techniques associated with technological advancement and knowledge domain which includes the facts and figures related to the work that an employee can access. Srivastava (2015) in the paper states that competency mapping acts as a flow chart for determining future Human Resource Strategy for any organization.

Shree et al(2016) evaluated the competency of the employees of the tyre industry. The paper stated that competency is something that describes how a job might be done excellently. Competence only describes what has to be done and not how it has to be done. Core competency is something which cannot be copied and it is the pillar upon which individual rests. One of the first encounters with competencies for most individuals is in securing employment in a new association that are intentionally using cutting-edge methods to choose talent for positions or project roles are engaging in what is called ‘ competency based interview & determination’. Later these are utilized as to evaluate execution, to support future improvement plans from individuals and to plan for succession in the company. Shah (2016) experimented the extent to which the various competencies related to a job are possessed by a job holder and viewed that competency mapping is a process used by an HR expert to identify and list out competencies that are most relevant and significant to carry out job in an effective manner. Most popular strategies used by companies to map the competencies include core competencies required for company’s success, competency sets, position specific competency sets and competency sets defined for each job holder. Once the identification of competencies is done, competency profiling is prepared which will set the expected key competencies for a job. Expected or required competencies are matched against the actual competencies of a job holder. The process of identifying the gap between expected and actual competencies is referred to as Competency Mapping.

Bharadwajet. al (2019) in the paper identifies ability advancement as a competent technique for raising the productivity of the small and medium scale industries. The components of ability advancement includes technical, managerial, communication skills, negotiation, team spirit, concern for excellence at work, emotional intelligence, coaching and mentoring, etc. Statistical analysis such as ANOVA suggests that technical skills, managerial competencies, time management, communication skills, behavioral competency does not have any impact on the productivity of the company.

Manjuet. al (2020) in the paper discusses the effectiveness of Competency Mapping in the Ites sector, analyses the skills with respect to employee development and alignment of behaviour of employees with organizational strategies. The goals and requirements of the company have been assessed by competency mapping, levelling the benchmarks, employee motivation for better job performance, employee performance, skill gap and its remedies, accepting the challenges that are achievable which measures the effectiveness and efficiency of the employees.

Waikeret. al(2022) in the paper discussed the continuous demand for high skilled and knowledge based jobs is putting more pressure on the employees to be more competitive and adaptable. Identifying the right talent is a herculean task from the organizational point of view from the set of skills that are required for any job. This creates a necessity for job analysis, job specification and staff selection in any organization. Skill crisis is a matter of concern for organization these days according to a study conducted by Deloitte, 39% of the employees are not able to meet their talent needs resulting in either outsourcing their task to other companies or growth inside the market.

As today's organizations are getting more competitive oriented, any competency gets obsolete very fast with the coming of new competencies. This paper identifies 11 crucial competencies which are looked upon by organizations during placement and selection. These competencies include willingness to learn, achievement orientation, concern for order, quality and accuracy, energy, passion, self-confidence, team work, cooperation, analytical thinking, technical expertise, customer service, initiative, problem-solving, etc. The paper analyses that critical thinking and problem solving are two skill deficit the students are facing and this gap should be filled up by the academicians apart from imparting knowledge as per their curriculum. The focus is thus more on employability education. (Aralihond and Battur, 2020)

In any challenging and volatile competitive environment, competition arises in terms of providing products at reduced costs, good quality with higher performance, product flexibility, etc. Thus, organisations are trying to improve their core competencies which will give an edge over the competitors in the fast changing market requirements. (Ajitabh and Mohmaya, 2004). Hamel and Prahalad(1994) defined core competencies as a set of skills and technologies beneficial to the customers. Core competencies provides the basis for good quality products and services. Competitive competencies are the need of the hour (Erin, 2004). Singh, Garg and Deshmukh (2008) finds the secret of sustainable development lies in core competencies that are irreplaceable. New technologies and recognising the market changes are considered to be most important competencies because they are related with subjective, objective and overall competitiveness of the organisation. Knowledge, understanding, values and skills taken together is considered to be a holistic approach to competency. Professional competencies are the sum total of cognitive competencies, functional competencies, personal competencies, ethical competencies and meta competencies (Makulova et.al, 2015)

2.4 Competency Mapping in Banking Sector

Aziz (2005) emphasised that banking is a knowledge intensive, skill-based and relationship-rich industry. In a progressive, complex and a more liberalized environment, competitiveness of banks will depend significantly on the quality of human resource and the extent to which the industry is able to enhance these talents. To compete effectively, banking institutions need professionals with the ample skills and expertise at all functional areas. Thus, the banking sector gives more priority to strengthen their intellectual human resources and the competency of them. Indian banking organizations are also witnessing a change in systems, management cultures and philosophy due to the global alignment of Indian organizations. There is a need for multi skill development. In this connection, Sharma & Khanna (2015) highlighted that competency mapping analyses an individual's SWOT which helps to improve in his career and helps to identify the gap that exists between actual and desired competencies. The study found that competency mapping is not only done for confirmed employees of an organization but can also be done for contract workers or for those seeking employment to emphasize the specific skills which would make them valuable to a potential employer. These kinds of skills can be determined when one is ready to do the work. Hence, competency mapping is one of the most accurate means in identifying the job and behavioural competencies of an individual in an organization.

As global business competition shifts from efficiency to innovation and from enlargement of scale to creation of value, management needs to be oriented towards the strategic use of human resources. In this context, Kaur and Kumar (2013) tested the extent of competency mapping that would help in analyzing the gap in required skill and could be worked upon to improve the level of competency. The competencies of managers from three different levels of management were measured with the help of questionnaire and gap was analyzed. The study concluded that the manager in higher level lacked in technical skills compared to middle level manager. Planning skills and leadership skill were missing in middle and first level. The implementation of competency mapping would focus on the gap that are essential for the required job and hence can be improved by training which will further enhance the organization effectiveness and facilitates the organization to meet its business objectives. Nair (2014) asserted that to compete effectively, banking institutions need professionals with the requisite skills and expertise not only at the strategic and management level, but also at the technical and operational levels and strengthening the employees' competency is the only possible solution by which the banks can determine its future growth. Kumar et. al (2014) conducts a study on 5 branches of HDFC Bank Ltd. in Amritsar This paper identifies the perception of the employees regarding competency mapping, analyses the different activities where competency mapping is proved to be beneficial, identifies the effective measures and determines the core competencies required for the leaders, managers and associate managers. The responses collected depicts that 37% agree that competencies are essential prerequisites that contribute to the effective performance of the bank employees. Customer focus, team orientation, communication, result orientation, adaptability, leadership and innovation are the core competencies that have been identified for the managerial level of the employees. Majority of the employees are satisfied with the working environment of the banks which are beneficial for their working environment. The bankers are on a consensus that training programs are of utmost importance for the competency development of the employees and should be systematic aand scientific on their approach. More than 70% of the respondents agree that competency assessment is also required for manpower planning, recruitment, selection, career development and promotion. Therefore, job analysis is of utmost importance and the corresponding competencies to perform the job. Well-structured training programs that consists contents on knowledge, skills and abilities should be conducted. The employees are also of the view that there should be specific training about the changes occurring in the banking industry.

Chandekar and Jain (2015)opined that competencies are enhanced through training and job rotation. Job rotation acts as a learning experience for the employees and it widens their horizon about the company itself. To do all this effectively and efficiently, competency mapping for each recruitment cycle will ease the work, resulting in proper selection as per criteria found from mapping and assessment so that employees will know their job and can perform more independently and thereby the employee morale will be boost up. Murtaza (2015) attempted to identify the gap between the competencies present and the competencies that are required for the employees in the tourism department to function at its best which helps the employees to understand the process and requirements of the department more effectively and thus will be of direct help to develop the training schedule of the employees in such a way that the training program suits better to meet the employee's and departmental needs.

The paper also measures where this gap can be filled. Based on this, a competency map was developed which was handful in suggesting improvements for the tourism sector.Choudhary and Singh (2016) studied on competency mapping of employees of banking sector in the context of changing business environment. The paper identified the need of competency mapping in various business areas and conducted a survey on competency mapping in banking sector. It attempts to measure the role of competency mapping in the efficient performance of the employees at middle level and determine various functional areas, where the competency mapping can be proved beneficial. The research of study based on primary data collected from the different branches of ICICI bank, located at different place in Agra. The result of the study has proved that the competency mapping is necessary for the performance and future growth of banks because the growth and development of every business is based on the efficient and satisfied working staff.

An insight into IBM Analytics Datasheet (2016) gives us a description of the skills and competencies required for banking and financial services. Kenexa Talent Frameworks is an IBM based outsourcing company which looks upon the competencies and skills of potential employees across 18 different industries. The company also makes cloud based software for analyzing employees job skills and competencies, self-assessment of employees and managers, skill gap analysis, etc. The study states that right skills and talent may save from adverse risk management issues such as product innovation, regulatory compliance, sales, customer service, industry consolidation, mergers and acquisitions, retail and investment issues, etc. Competency Framework may answer many critical questions like skills required to support new product, recruit the best talent for benchmarking the performance standards, maximize revenues by understanding the new web dynamic social trends, critical knowledge required for boosting institutional memory, integration of best resources to maximize investment. The company defines an architectural framework for Banking and Finance companies. The skills and competencies of the employees should depend on the job profile. The goals, interview questions, coaching tips and learning resources are considered as performance accelerators which impacts the behavior of the employees. The types of skills and competencies identified are core competencies, leadership and management, business, interpersonal, job functional, job technical, task specific etc.

Mohankumari and Magesh (2017) highlighted that competencies provide organizations with a way to define in behavioural terms what it is that people need to do to produce the results that the organization desires to keep with its culture. Competencies allow organizations to analyse the extent to which behaviours of employees are to be demonstrated. This will allow organizations to know what resources they may need to help the employee development and learn those competencies.While two organizations may be alike in financial results, the way in which the results were achieve could be different based on the competencies that fit their particular strategy and organizational culture. Competencies can provide a structured model that can be used to integrate management practices throughout the organization.

Technological advancement in the banking sector has compelled the organizations to minimize expenditure on human resources and upgrade its resources to skilled labourers without compromising its productivity. The e-commerce platforms like e-recruitment, e-selection, e-training, e-compensation, etc. are adopted by the banks to work in a competitive environment. Improvement in human quality and development in human skills, standards, comprehension and application in the production departments are in paramount importance.

Customer relationship is of prime importance in the banking industry and the satisfaction of the customers determine the fate of the banking sector. The paper analyses a case study on private and public sector banks where it was found that personnel management practices and proactive communications led to a decrease in performance of private sector banks.

Talent crunch and skill shortage have compelled the banks to focus more on internal customers as equally as external customers. Thus private sector banks focuses more on training and thus competency mapping is essential to point out the grey areas that requires training and mentoring. Performance appraisal is not up to the mark as compared to public sector banks. Job satisfaction, recruitment and retention, career growth depends on the competencies of the employees. (Fatmaand Mishra,2017)

2.5 Job Description and Competency

Landy, Shankster-Cawley and Moran (1995) in the 1940's mentioned the focus of job description and job analysis was task centric with very less emphasis to employee attributes. McCormick, Jeanneret and Mecham (1969) developed an approach called Position Analysis Questionnaire (PAQ) which was more employee centric and included more focus on the employees. PAQ focused on qualities, traits and skills needed for job analysis and the competencies aligned to that. With flexible organizational structures, task based job descriptions are being replaced by employee-centric job descriptions. (Schippmann,2010)

Lawler and Ledford (1992); Nybo, (2004) and Pavur, (2010) pointed out the important human resource decisions such as selection, training, career development, pay determination and promotion are determined by the job description in an organization. Stybel (2010) highlighted the contents of job description include job title, reporting relationships, list of responsibilities, authorized decision-making and hiring requirement information. Lawler (1984) found out that the employees can be motivated to perform their duties efficiently by aligning a well-defined job description. Strategic human resource management has directed the use of competency based job descriptions more prominent. (Hawkes and Weathington, 2014).

Lawler (1994) pointed out that job descriptions help to rationalize the overall structure of the organization. Bodnarchuk(2012) stated that job analysis collects information about the job to find out the similarities and differences. For this purpose job analysis uses questionnaire to gather information on input, mental processes, work output, relationship with other persons, job context and job related variables (Bratton, 2007). Job description helps to analyse where an employee stands in the organisation.

2.6 Knowledge as a Parameter in Competency Mapping

Sinha, Sinha and Singh (2016) in the paper states that competency mapping identifies the core competencies in an organization that deserves highest importance and so every organization should have systematic set roles roles defined for the betterment of the employees. It identifies emplyees strengths and weaknesses which helps him in his career. It was also identified that communication and the knowledge levels of the employees, if improved can lead to more competent employees in an organization.

Assessment of competencies in an impartial manner in HCL Technologies, Chennai led to the identification of the gap between present competencies and expected competencies of the employees. The research also brought out the influence of gender on the level of competencies possessed by the employees and t-test analysis revealed that there is significant level of difference between two sets of gender on the basis of personal effectiveness, functional expertise, innovation, personal care, analytical thinking and motivation. (Velayudhan and Maran, 2009)

Boucher, Bonjour, Matta (2007) in the research emphasized that the era of globalization considers the management of human capital to be a strategic objective and the knowledge and skills proved to be essential key factors in developing the competencies of the human capital. The paradigm shift in the IT sector made it important to use knowledge intensive techniques in product designing. The knowledge intensive activities concerns the management of knowledge, skill and competence which act as competency drivers for efficient performance.

Berio and Harzallah (2007) in the study envisaged a parallel relationship between compence management and knowledge management. The paper states that how knowledge engineering can support competency building activities.

Knowledge Management refers to the development, storage, retrieval and dissemination of information. Knowledge is required both for competition as well as for innovation. Knowledge Management helps in dynamic learning, problem solving and strategic planning.

Knowledge can be categorized as tacit and explicit knowledge. Tacit knowledge refers to subjective, objective and experiential learning whereas explicit knowledge refers to objective, rational and technical knowledge. KM coverts tacit to explicit knowledge using the various KM methodologies. (Nonaka and Takeuchi, 1995). The criticism that beholds KM is regarding the value it imparts to the organization and how CEOs are making the right use of it. (Gupta, Iyer, Aronson, 2000).

The knowledge based firms such as banks strongly consider the implementation of the Knowledge Management practices in the firm and it is seen that all the respondents who are being encountered are aware of the concept. The views of the respondents are aligned with the fact that the knowledge management practices in the branches of the bank is in a growing stage, the first parameter was the practices adopted in knowledge sharing, where as the second, third, fourth and fifth being knowledge transfer, store knowledge, knowledge creation, organizational learning and culture. Therefore, the need for Knowledge Management practices are increasing and the employees should be aware of this concept and it should be practiced in the organization for better performance in jobs.(Chakravorty and Ahmed, 2020)

Hu (2019) in the paper envisaged Knowledge employees in e-commerce companies are individuals with advanced degrees, better knowledge and technological capabilities, a strong aptitude for learning. Through their inventive thinking, innovative spirits can help e-commerce businesses appreciate their knowledge capital. In the paper, two categories of knowledge-based workers in e-commerce companies are identified. One is knowledge-based management staff, such as market workers and e-commerce operators, who possess great leadership, organization, coordination, control, and innovative skills.The other group consists of knowledge workers with a focus on technology, including engineers, designers, and other professionals involved in information technology research.The definition of knowledge staff for e-commerce businesses indicates that these workers differ from regular workers in that they have a strong sense of education, adaptability, decision-making skills for their careers, a strong capacity for learning and innovation, resilience, a strong ability to work in a team, strong communication skills, a focus on pursuing self-realization, clear career planning with room for growth, etc.

2.7 Skills as a Parameter of Competency Mapping

A developed nation's ability to retain and enhance healthy competition, particularly amongst industries, is largely dependent on its labor force, which is a critical component. Therefore, having a trained workforce is one way to achieve a sustainable nation and provide a technological labor force for the job market of the future (Ayonmike, Okwelle, and Okeke, 2014).

The workplace has transformed at a rate never seen before. Thanks to the success of new digital technology. According to Ishak (2016) a great deal of confusion has been created by the Industrial Revolution 4.0. Thus, according to some analysts, this shift will result in the elimination of some employment and the creation of new ones (Rajnai & Kocsis, 2017). All of the contentious talks about Industrial Revolution 4.0 and digital transformation are more in line with the need to create suitable concepts for professional certification and training, particularly vocational training (Ahmad, 2016). Because of this, the central idea would center on the issue of determining which competency will be necessary in the future and how to acquire the necessary skill.

Chakravorty and Ahmed (2022) pointed that for leadership roles, especially those in middle and top management, conceptual skills are crucial. It is the managers' responsibility to ensure that all employees are contributing to the company's objectives. Upper and medium level managers must remember the company's objectives in addition to becoming mired in the minutiae of everyday tasks. Thus, conceptual abilities are helpful in practically any role. Competency assessment measures a person's ability based on the requirements of his or her employment. It is not necessary to excel at every work in order to be competent in a productive setting; rather, one must master the abilities and competences that are essential to one's success.

Digitization is a hallmark of a technologically disruptive era in many people's lives. In addition to its advantages, the fourth industrial revolution presents obstacles that need to be overcome. When a nation implements the 4.0 industrial revolution, it faces challenges such as resistance to changes in social and demographic aspects, political instability, resource scarcity, natural disaster risk, and demands for the use of environmentally friendly technology. The PESTEL framework serves as the foundation for analysing difficulties in the context of the fourth industrial revolution by taking into account political, economic, social, technological, environmental, and legal factors. Individual attitudes, drive, and social ideals are all components of personal competence. HR functions well in the community when it is supported by new literacy, leadership, teamwork, mental maturity and character, culture, and entrepreneurship. (Damayanti, 2021)

Katz's model, which emphasizes the value of not just technical proficiency but also the capacity to work with and through people, as well as the ability to think strategically and comprehend complex organizational dynamics, has been crucial in guiding the understanding of managerial roles and skills. (S. El-Sabaa, 1999). It has been noted that among project managers, human skills are most influential, whereas technical abilities are least. To work and function, a project manager needs to comprehend cross-functional relationships. In order to succeed, interpersonal skills are crucial. (Panwar and Sati,2023)

2.8 Self –concept as a Parameter of Competency Mapping

Prof. Charles Horton Cooley developed the concept of "Looking Glass-self' in his famous work, 'Human Nature and the Order' in the year 1902. This theory is basically a process of description on how they believe others view them.Nebo (2022) in the paper describes the concept of the 'Looking Glass Self' and its implication in leadership development. 'Looking Glass Self' is considered a solution to the leadership problem. This concept sets as a mirror in which the leader rethinks how he appears and how he is evaluated in the eyes of his followers. The feedback received from the followers helps in leader's self-development. The paper concludes that although the leaders listen to the comments of the followers, it is completely on the leader's biasness as to how the leaders interpret the follower's perception.

Hughes, Galbraith and White (2011) in their research pointed out that self-efficacy and self-concept both contain a common element called as perceived competence. The components of self-concept are both affective perception and competence perception.(Marsh,1992). Pajares and Schunk(2002) in the framework pointed out that self-concept reciprocates on oneself and asks 'being' questions. E.g. "Am I good at Mathematics?" Skaalvick(1997) focuses on the cognitive dimension of self-concept as descriptive (I am a good person) and evaluative (How well am I doing?) Self-schema is a sum total of all the components of self-concept which includes belief in one's abilities, roles, skills, experiences and characteristics. (Jerslid, 1965; Marsh &Shavelson, 1985; West & Fish, 1973).

Marsh, Walker and Debus (1991) in their research opined that the judgment on self-concept are more general and environmental experiences, social and self-comparisons. The perception of self-concept are also based on previous experiences. The perceptions in self –concept are seen as habitual and recurring in nature. (Goetz, Cronjaeger, Frenzel, Ludtke, and Hall, 2010).

Pietsch,Walker, and Chapman(2003) researched that self-concept are examined at the same level of specificity i.e. subject or task specific. Baumiester (1991) defines self-concept as the totality of inferences a person has made about himself or herself. Individuals with positive self-concept accepts themselves positively and readily accept their identity. Judge et.al (1997) points out that core self-evaluation is a personality construct comprised of dimensions like self-esteem, generalized self –efficacy, non-neuroticism, locus of control, etc.

2.9 Traits as a Parameter of Competency Mapping

The Big Five Personality Theory is among the widely accepted personality models accepted all over the world in research context. Research from the past predicts that this model has been a predictor of behavior irrespective of all situations. (Abzari et al., 2016). There has been several evidences from literature that personality has been as a predictor of work performance Competencies. Banking sector has always been in the forefront among the service sector due to its impeccable contribution in the financial sector. The frontline employees are the first hand service providers and are solely responsible for customer satisfaction and increasing the credibility of the bank.(Gustaffson,2009; Burmann and Konig, 2011; Fang et al., 2015). The employees need to work in a multi-faceted work environment and therefore have to focus on enriching the competencies to meet the diversified work culture. Hu, Li and Song (2023) identified the key competencies, the personality traits and the psychological capital with a focus on personality and increasing the psychological capital among college students. The findings provide a link between agreeableness, conscientiousness, emotional stability, extroversion and openness to experience and the competency required for the college students.

Costa and McCrae (2008) extensively researched the Big Five Personality model and briefly explains each of the traits. Agreeableness measures personal harmony, trust, straight forwardness, altruism, modesty and tenderness. Conscientiousness refers to organization skills and responsibility, emotional stability implies whether you are stable, depressed or irritable. Extroversion implies sociable and outgoing, followed by warmth, gregariousness and positive emotions. Openness to experience refers to receptive to new ideas, feelings, intellectual curiosity, etc.

Barrick, Mount and Judge (1991) extended the relationship between Big Five Personality models and job performance at work. The findings indicated that 'conscientiousness' has maintained stable relationship with all the indicators of job performance.

Bartram(2005); Kanfer and Ackerman (2005) pointed out in their studies that competencies are predicted in traits. Personality dimensions are indicators of effective work behaviors, namely generic competencies applied to all professions. Since traits are considered to be the indicators of behavioral patterns then competencies sets the limits for how individual potentialities may turn to effective organizational behaviors.(Spencer and Spencer, 2008)

Chakravorty and Ahmed (2024) in the paper aimed to find out the impact of Big Five Personality traits on the competencies of Axis, HDFC and ICICI Banks of North East India. The results indicate that HDFC and Axis Banks are more competent than ICICI Banks in all the parameters of Personality.

2.10 Motives as a Parameter of Competency Mapping

Schulz and Steyn (2003) describe about the understanding the concept of motives will help move the employees to act.

Herzberg"s motivation–hygiene theory or two-factor theory is one of the prominent theories of motivation that has received widespread recognition of all times.

Responses about good feelings were categorized as motivators (satisfiers) and bad feelings as hygiene factors (dissatisfiers). He further categorized motivators under achievement, recognition, responsibility, advancement, possibility of growth and the work itself which are intrinsic in nature. Hygiene factors were classified under interpersonal relationships with supervisors, peers and subordinates, salary, status, job security, personal life, technical supervision, working conditions and company policy and administration, which are extrinsic to the working conditions. (Prasad, 2015).

Responses about good feelings were categorized as motivators (satisfiers) and bad feelings as hygiene factors (dissatisfiers). He further categorized motivators under achievement, recognition, responsibility, advancement, possibility of growth and the work itself which are intrinsic in nature. Hygiene factors were classified under interpersonal relationships with supervisors, peers and subordinates, salary, status, job security, personal life, technical supervision, workingconditions and company policy and administration, which are extrinsic to the working conditions. (Prasad, 2015) excellence, incentive linked schemes etc. were responsible for low levels of motivation. The banking sector did not prioritise the motivation of employees through the development of soft skills, oral communication, good working conditions and non-monetary benefits. (Shannon, 2005). With the emergence of private sector banks, the organisations could not have rigid control over the organizations. The employees realized that the major source of fulfilment of motivation could not be only through the fulfilment of basic needs. The banking sector has realized that once the employee is motivated, the customers are served well which in turn increases the profitability and accountability of the organization. This circle of excellence is of prime importance in customer centric business processes that we are witnessing in banking today and more so in the years to come.

Chakravorty, Ahmed and Chakrabarty(2023) in the research points inthe toils put in by the bankers during the recent demonetization policy to cool down the havoc spread across the country is just an exemplification of the stress they go through during phases of such policy execution. The research is intended to tap into the factors responsible for keeping up the motivation level of the employees in carrying out their hectic work roles. The bankers need to have more diverse approaches in dealing with people of different sets of customers.

The roles of the bankers in dealing with such sceptic customers become much more complex. The research undermines the framework provided by the Herzberg model in explaining the factors sustaining and enhancing the motivation level of the workforce in any organizational set-up and applies the same in the research. Hygiene set of factors passed through the ANOVA analysis where it was discovered that there was no variation in the level of influence of the factors in sustaining the job satisfaction of the employees. The second phase of analysis discovered that there was a significant variation in the level of influence of the motivators.

2.11 Research Gap

The underpinning of the above literature in the context of competency mapping helps us to understand the meaning of competency and its associated terms. The competitiveness of banks in an advanced, sophisticated, and more liberalized environment will be greatly influenced by the calibre of human resources and the degree to which the sector is able to develop these abilities. Banking organizations require personnel with a wide range of skills and competence across all functional areas in order to compete effectively. As a result, the banking industry places greater emphasis on enhancing the intellectual capital and capability of its workforce. Because of their worldwide alignment, Indian banking businesses are also seeing changes in their management cultures, processes, and philosophy and thus the identification and development of multiple skills is necessary.

References

Abzari, M., Shahin, A., & Abasaltian, A. (2016). Studying the impact of personality constructs on employees' knowledge sharing behavior through considering the mediating role of intelligent competencies in project-oriented organizations. *Modern Applied Science*, *10*(6), 194-204.

Ahmad, Z. (2016). *Education 2030 Launch and Symposium. Malaysia Ministry of Education, (August)*. Retrieved from https://www.moe.gov.my/images/Terbitan/Rujukan-Akademik/Presentation-Education-2030-Launch-Symposium-23rd-August-2016-Hotel-Istana-Ballroom-Kuala-Lumpur/Zanariah-Hj-Ahmad/Zanariah Hj. Ahmad.pdf

Ajitabh, A., & Momaya, K. (2004). Competitiveness of firms: review of theory, frameworks and models. *Singapore management review*, *26*(1), 45-61.

Aralihond, T. and Battur, A. (2020). A Study on Competency Mapping of B-School Students For Employability. *International E Conference on Adapting to the New Business Normal – The way ahead December 3-4, 2020 Mysuru, India.*

Atkinson, S.P. (2015). Graduate Competencies, Employability and Educational Taxonomies: Critique of Intended Learning Outcomes. *Practice and Evidence of Scholarship of Teaching and Learning in Higher Education, 10*(2), 154-177.

Ayonmike, C. S. O., Chijioke, P., & Okeke, B. C. (2014). Competency based education and training in technical vocational education: Implication for sustainable national security and development. *Journal of Educational Policy and Entrepreneurial Research*, *1*(2), 290-300.

Aziz, Z.A. (2005). *Developing a robust competency framework for the Malaysian banking industry Opening speech by Dr Zeti Akhtar Aziz,* Governor of the Central Bank of Malaysia, at the Industry Competency Framework Study Focus Group Discussion, Kualaumpur, 6 December 2005. BIS Review 83/2005

Barrick, M. R., Mount, M. K., & Judge, T. A. (2001). Personality and performance at the beginning of the new millennium: What do we know and where do we go next?. *International Journal of Selection and assessment*, *9*(1-2), 9-30.

Bartram, D. (2005). The Great Eight competencies: a criterion-centric approach to validation. *Journal of applied psychology*, *90*(6), 1185.

Bath, D., Smith, C., Stein, C. and Swann, R. (2004). Beyond mapping and embedding graduate attributes: bringing together quality assurance and action learning to create a validated and living curriculum., *Higher Education Research & Development, 23*(3), 313-328.

Berio, G., &Harzallah, M. (2007). Towards an integrating architecture for competence management. *Computers in Industry*, *58*(2), 199-209.

Bharadwaj. et.al (2019). Competency Mapping Based on Identifying the Impact over the Productivity of SMEs. International Journal of Innovative Technology and Exploring Engineering (IJITEE), *9*(2), 2236.

Bodnarchuk, M. (2012). The role of job descriptions and competencies in an international organization: Case: Foster Wheeler EnergiaOy.

Boucher, X., Bonjour, E. and Matta, N. (2007). Competence Management in Industrial Processes. *Computers in Industry*. *58*(2), 95-97

Boyatzis, R. E. (1982). *The Competent Manager: A Model for Effective Performance*. New Delhi: New Age International Private Limited.

Boyatzis, R. E. (1982). *The Competent Manager: A Model for Effective Performance*. New Delhi: New Age International Private Limited.

Boyatzis, R.E. (2009), "Competencies as a behavioral approach to emotional intelligence", Journal of Management Development, Vol. 28, No. 9,

Boyatzis, R. E (2007) Competencies in the 21st century, *Journal of Management Development, 27* (1), 5-12.

Bratton, J. (2007). Strategic human resource management. *Human Resource Management içinde, Der: John Bratton,-Gold, Jeffrey, London: Palgrave Macmillan, London,* 37-71.

Bücker, J., &Poutsma, E. (2010). Global management competencies: A theoretical foundation. *Journal of Managerial Psychology, 25*(8), 829-844.

Burmann, C., & König, V. (2011). Does internal brand management really drive brand commitment in shared-service call centers? *Journal of brand management, 18*(6), 374-393.

Chakravorty, D. and Ahmed, J.U. (2020). Knowledge Management as a parameter of Competency Mapping: A Study in HDFC Bank Ltd. Operating at Silchar, Assam. In Akoijam, S.L.S, Sharma, L. S, Ahmed, J.U. and Singh, W.C. (Eds), *Dynamics of Sustainable Business Management: Perspectives and Strategies* (pp. 229-242). Mittal Publications

Chakravorty, D. and Ahmed, J.U. (2024). The Influence of Big Five Personality Traits on the Competencies of the Bank Employees: A Study on Private Bank Employees of North East India. *ISAR Journal of Economics and Business Management, 2*(2), 1-7. https://isarpublisher.com/journal/isarjebm

Chakravorty, D. and Ahmed, J.U.(2022). Competitive Banking Environment: A Study on Private Sector Banks in Tura Region of Meghalaya. In Kakati, R.P. and Mahanta, M. (Eds), *Business Practices in the Age of Innovation, Disruption and Sustainability, 2*, (pp. 115-119*)*. Excel Publishers

Chakravorty, D., Ahmed, J. U. and Chakravarty, D. (2023). Assessing Herzberg's Theory in Private Banking: A Competency Study. *International Journal of Science and Research (IJSR), 12*(12), 58-63. https://dx.doi.org/10.21275/SR231124183219

Chandekar, M and Jain, S.K. (2015). Competency Mapping: A Strategic tool in employee Recruitment. *Abhinav International Monthly Refereed Journal of Research in Management & Technology, 4*(1), 27-33

Currie, G. & Darby, R. (1995), "Competence-based Management Development: Rhetoric & Reality", Journal of European Industrial Training, Vol. 19, No. 5.

Damayanti, D. (2021). Human resources competency in the era of industrial revolution 4.0. *Economics and Business Solutions Journal, 5*(1), 13-27.

Fang, R., Landis, B., Zhang, Z., Anderson, M. H., Shaw, J. D., & Kilduff, M. (2015). Integrating personality and social networks: A meta-analysis of personality, network position, and work outcomes in organizations. *Organization science, 26*(4), 1243-1260.

Fatma, A. and Mishra, M.K. (2017). Analytical Study of Competency Mapping and Employees Effectiveness of Private Banks in Urban Jhansi. *Journal of Advances and Scholarly Researches in Allied Education, 13*(1), 1124-1126.

Garrett, S. (2008). *Competency Mapping: What Is It and How It Can Be Done by Individuals*. Career Trainer

Goetz, T., Cronjaeger, H., Frenzel, A. C., Ludtke, O., & Hall, N. C. (2010). Academic self-concept and emotion relations: Domain specificity and age effects. *Contemporary Educational Psychology, 35*, 44-58.

Gupta, B., Iyer, L.S. and Aronson, J.E. (2000). Knowledge Management: Practices and Challenges. *Industrial Management and Data Systems, 100*(1), 17-21

Hawkes, C. L., &Weathington, B. L. (2014). Competency-Based Versus Task-Based Job Descriptions: Effects on Applicant Attraction. Journal of Behavioral and Applied Management, 15(3), 190-211.

Hayes, J.L. (1979). A new look at managerial competence: the AMA model of worthy performance. *Management Review, 68*(11), 2-3.

Hind, D., Moss, S. and McKellan, S. (2007). Innovative Assessment Strategies for developing Employability Skills in the Tourism and Entertainment Management Curriculum at Leeds Metropolitan University.Paper presented at the Euro-CHRIE Conference, Leeds, UK.

Hu, A., Li, X., & Song, H. (2023). The influence of Big Five personality traits on college students' key competencies: the mediating effect of psychological capital. *Frontiers in Psychology, 14*.

Hu, Q. (2019, February). Analysis on the Impact of Knowledge-based Employees' Competency on Performance in E-commerce Enterprises. In *2018 International Symposium on Social Science and Management Innovation (SSMI 2018)* (pp. 545-552). Atlantis Press.

Hughes, A., Galbraith, D., & White, D. (2011). Perceived competence: A common core for self-efficacy and self-concept?. *Journal of personality assessment, 93*(3), 278-289.

IBM Analytics Datasheet(2016). Banking and Fiancial Services. Job Skills and Competencies Framework. https://www.redbooks.ibm.com/redbooks/pdfs/sg247908.pdf

Ishak, H. (2016). Industrial Revolution 4.0 in Malaysia? "Fostering Research and Malaysian Aerospace Industry. *Factory of The Future*.

Jerslid, A. T. (1965). Social and original origins of the self. In D. E. Hamachek (Ed.), *The self in growth, teaching and learning* (pp. 196-208). Englewood Cliffs.

Judge, T. A., Martocchio, J. J., & Thoresen, C. J. (1997). Five-factor model of personality and employee absence. *Journal of applied psychology, 82*(5), 745.

Kanfer, R., & Ackerman, P. L. (2005). Work competence. *Handbook of competence and motivation*, 336-353.

Klemp, G.O. (ed.) (1980). *The Assessment of occupational competence,* Washington, DC, Report to National Institution of Education.

Kumar, S., Nayyar, S. and Anjuman, B. (2014). Competency Mapping - A Managerial Perception (A Study Of Hdfc Bank Ltd. *Journal of Social Science Research*. 3. 373-384

Lawler III, E. E. (1994). From job-based to competency-based organizations. *Journal of organizational behavior*, *15*(1), 3-15.

Lawler III, Edward, E. (1994). From job-based to competency-based organizations. *Journal of organizational behavior*, *15*(1), 3-15.

Lawler, E. E. (1984). The strategic design of reward systems. *Strategic human resource management*, *9*(1), 7-16.

Makulova, A. T., Alimzhanova, G. M., Bekturganova, Z. M., Umirzakova, Z. A., Makulova, L. T., & Karymbayeva, K. M. (2015). Theory and practice of competency-based approach in education. *International Education Studies*, *8*(8), 183-192.

Manju, S., Jayanthi, D. and Kowsalya, N. (2020). Competency Mapping Among TheItes Sectors: A Study Among The Ites Employees In Coimbatore. European Journal of Molecular & Clinical Medicine, *7*(3).

Marsh, H. W. (1992). Content specificity of relations between academic achievement and academic self-concept. *Journal of educational psychology*, *84*(1), 35.

Marsh, H. W., & Shavelson, R. (1985). Self-concept: Its multifaceted, hierarchical structure. *Educational Psychologist*, *20*, 107–125.

Marsh, H. W., Walker, R., & Debus, R. L. (1991). Subject-specific components academic self-concept and self-efficacy. *Contemporary Educational Psychology*, *16*, 331–345.

McClelland, D.C. (1973). Testing for competence rather than for intelligence. *American Psychologist, 28*(1), 1–14.

McCrae, R. R., & Costa, P. T. (2008). Empirical and theoretical status of the five-factor model of personality traits. *The SAGE handbook of personality theory and assessment*, *1*, 273-294.

Md. Ishtiak Uddin, et. al. (2012) Competency Mapping: A Tool for HR Excellence, European Journal of Business and Management, Vol. 4, No. 5.

Mohanakumari, D. and Magesh, R. (2017) Competency development through training and development: An empirical study, *Indian J.Sci. Res, 14* (1), 69-70.

Murtaza, Z. (2015) An Empirical Study of Competency Mapping of the Employees in the Tourism Sector in Jammu and Kashmir-An Executive Level Perespective. *Journal of Business Management & Social Sciences Research, 4*(2), 202-208

Nair, V.V. (2014) *Behavioural Competency Management with Special Reference To Commercial Banks Headquartered in Kerala* (Doctoral Dissertation, Cochin University of Science and Technology, Kerala, India)

Nebo, A. M. (2022). The application of "The Looking Glass Self" to leadership development. *Net Journal of Social Sciences, 10*(1), 12-18.

Nonaka, I and Takeuchi, H. (1995), The Knowledge-creating Company: How Japanese Companies Create the Dynamics of Innovation, Oxford University Press.

Nybø, G. (2004). Personnel development for dissolving jobs: towards a competency-based approach?. *The International Journal of Human Resource Management, 15*(3), 549-564.

Panwar, D., & Sati, M. C. (2023). Impact of Katz's Skills of Managers in School Management: A Study of Pauri District in Uttarakhand, India. *Migration Letters, 20*(S10), 508-513.

Parry, S.R. (1996). *The Quest for Competencies,* Training. *33*(7), 48-56.

Pavur Jr, E. J. (2010). Use job descriptions to support leadership. *The Psychologist-Manager Journal, 13*(2), 119-122.

Pietsch, J., Walker, R., & Chapman, E. (2003). The relationship among self-concept, self-efficacy, and performance in mathematics during secondary school. *Journal of Educational Psychology, 95*, 589–603.

Prahalad, C. K., & Hamel, G. (1994). Strategy as a field of study: Why search for a new paradigm? *Strategic management journal, 15*(S2), 5-16.

Prasad, P. (2015). Performance Appraisal: An Empirical Study to understand Job Satisfaction and Motivation of personnel through the system. International Journal of Engineering and Applied Sciences, 2(4), 118-125

Rainsbury, E., Hodges, D., Burchell, N. and Lay, M. (2002). Ranking Workplace Competencies: Student and Graduate Perceptions, *Asia-Pacific Journal of Cooperative Education, 3*(2), 8-18

Rajnai, Z., & Kocsis, I. (2017, September). Labor market risks of industry 4.0, digitization, robots and AI. In *2017 IEEE 15th International Symposium on Intelligent Systems and Informatics (SISY)* (pp. 000343-000346). IEEE.

S. El-Sabaa(2001).The Skills and Career Path of an Effective Project Manager. *International Journal of Project Management,19*, 1-7.

Schippmann, J. S. (2010). Competencies, job analysis, and the next generation of modeling. *Handbook of workplace assessment, 32*, 197

Schulz, S., & Steyn, T. (2003). Educators' motivation: Differences related to gender, age and experience. *Actaacademica, 35*(3), 138-160.

Schunk, D. H., & Pajares, F. (2002). The development of academic self-efficacy. In *Development of achievement motivation* (pp. 15-31). Academic Press.

Shannon, R. (2005). Herzberg's Two-Factor Theory of Motivation applied to the motivational techniques within financial institutions". Senior Honors Theses & Projects. 119

Singh, R. K., Garg, S. K., & Deshmukh, S. G. (2008). Competency and performance analysis of Indian SMEs and large organizations: An exploratory study. *Competitiveness Review: An International Business Journal, 18*(4), 308-321.

Sinha, D., Sinha, S., and Singh, K. (2016), Global HRM Review, Vol. 6, 86-94

Skaalvik, E. M. (1997). Self-enhancing and self-defeating ego orientation: Relations with task and avoidance orientation, achievement, self-perceptions, and anxiety. *Journal of educational psychology*, *89*(1), 71.

Spencer, L. M., & Spencer, P. S. M. (2008). *Competence at Work models for superior performance*. John Wiley & Sons.

Spencer, L.M and Spencer, S.M. (1993). *Competence at Work*. New York: Wiley

Stybel, L. J. (2010). Managing the inner contradictions of job descriptions: A technique for use in recruitment. *The Psychologist-Manager Journal, 13*(2), 105-110.

Tejaswari, A. and Ambuli, T.V (2016). A Study of Competency Mapping of Employees with Reference to Murugappan and Company.International Journal of Research Science and Management. *3*(8), 21-31

Tiwari (Mishra), S. (2012). Skills, Competencies and Employability Through Business Education. *AIMA Journal of Management & Research, 6*(4/4).

United Nations Industrial Development Organization. (2002). UNIDO Competencies. http://www.unido.org.

Velayudhan, M.T.K & Maran, K. (2009). A study on Mapping Core Competencies and development of Employees for Excellence with reference to HCL Technologies. *Journal of Contemporary Research in Management*, 53-67

Waiker, V., Siddiqui, M. A. A., & Ansari, M. S. A. (2022). A Review Study On Employees' Competency Mapping And Output Management: With Reference Nagpur Based Small Scale Manufacturing Industries. *Journal of Positive School Psychology*, *6*(7), 4105-4111.

West, C. K., & Fish, J. A. (1973). *Relationship between self-concept and school achievement: A survey of empirical investigations* (Final rep.). Urbana, IL:National Institute of Education

White, R. (1959). Motivation reconsidered: The concept competence. *Psychological Review, 66*(5), 279–333.

Worlikar, M. and Aggrawal, A. (2017). Review Study of Competency Mapping in the Organisations, *IOSR Journal of Business and Management,* 72-76.

Chapter - 3

Research Methodology

3.1 Introduction

This chapter highlights the objectives and methodology used in this research study. The purpose of this chapter is to provide scientifically prominent findings. This chapter is an elaboration of the detailed plan executed for this study. The objectives of the study determine the purpose of the research. The analytical tools that are used for the purpose of the study are described in this chapter.

3.2 Objectives of the Study

The objective of the study is to examine the competency mapping of bank employees of select private sector banks. The study will be progressed with the following objectives-

1. To study the job analysis conducted by banks in identifying the job description.
2. To examine the desired competencies as identified by the bank branch managers.
3. To measure the level of competencies possessed by the employees with regard to knowledge, skills, self-concept, traits and motives.

3.3 Hypothesis Framed

The following hypothesis has been framed to meet the objectives of the study.

There is no significant difference among the actual level of competencies and desired level of competencies across the banks.

3.4 Variables selected

To meet objective number one, the questionnaire was formulated to attain information about the job description based on Position Analysis Questionnaire (PAQ) developed by *McCormick, Jeanneret and Mecham (1969)*. The following parameters selected to measure the objective number one based on PAQ.

(a) Information input
(b) Mental Processes
(c) Work output
(d) Relationship with other persons
(e) Job context
(f) Job related variables

In order to meet the objective number two and three, the various dimensions of knowledge, skills, self-concept, traits and motives are identified based on Morey et al (2001), Robert Katz (1955), Goldberg (1990), Cooley (1902)and Herzberg's Two-Factor Theory (1959).

The parameters of knowledge have been selected for this study based on Morey *et al* (2001)

(a) Customer knowledge
(b) Knowledge in people
(c) Knowledge in products and services-
(d) Knowledge in process
(e) Organisational memory
(f) Knowledge in relationship
(g) Knowledge assets

The parameters of skills have been identified from managerial skills as identified by Katz (1955)

(a) Technical skills
(b) Human Skills
(c) Conceptual skills

The parameters of self -concept has been taken from the concept of Charles Horton Cooley's Looking glass self. (1902). The parameter has three principle elements:

(a) The imagination of our appearance to the other person
(b) The imagination of his judgment of that appearance
(c) Some sort of self-feeling such as pride or mortification

The parameters for traits have been identified fromGoldberg's (1990) trait theory.

(a) Agreeableness
(b) Conscientiousness
(c) Emotional stability
(d) Extroversion
(e) Introversion
(f) Openness

The parameters for motives have been identified from Herzberg's Two-Factor Theory (White, R.,1959)

Hygiene Factors (extrinsic factors)

(a) Company policy and administration
(b) Technical supervision
(c) Interpersonal relationship with supervisors
(d) Interpersonal relationship with peers
(e) Interpersonal relationship with subordinates
(f) Salary
(g) Job security
(h) Personal life
(i) Working Condition
(j) Status

Motivational Factors (intrinsic factors)

(a) Achievement
(b) Recognition
(c) Advancement

(d) Work itself

(e) Possibility of growth

(f) Responsibility

3.5 Research Design

The research design formulated is both descriptive and empirical research. It is descriptive because the relevant job descriptions in Objective Number 1 is identified through summary statistics by showing the responses to all possible questionnaire items and identifying its characteristics. Objective 1 also leads us in identifying the relevant jobs needed in job analysis through the items mentioned under Position Analysis Questionnaire (PAQ) developed by McCormick, Jeanneret and Mecham (1969).The responses have been collected on the following dimensions: Information input, Mental Processes, Work output, Relationship with other persons, Job context, and Job related variables.

The research is also empirical in nature because Objective 2 and Objective 3 uses inferential statistics to derive the results. It emphasizes on hypotheses formulation and tests its significance. The study also uses Iceberg Model of Competency model and considers its parameters to derive the results.

3.6 Data Collection

The research envisaged to use both primary and secondary data to derive the findings. Primary data was collected from the frontline employees of Axis, HDFC and ICICI Bank Ltd. from the seven states of North East India, namely, Assam, Meghalaya, Arunachal Pradesh, Tripura, Manipur, Mizoram and Nagaland through a structured questionnaire. Sikkim was excluded in this studyas the regional offices of these above mentioned banks falls under Kolkata Cluster for Sikkim.

3.7 Questionnaire Formulation

Three sets of questionnaire were formed keeping the sequence of the objectives of the study. The first set of Questionnaire was circulated to all the employees of the banks taken under consideration for identifying the job description. From the questionnaire, the major job functions are identified and then the skills required to perform each of the major job functions are listed. The second set of questionnaire was prepared for collecting the responses from the managers for measuring the importance of the competency parameters listed for the study. The third set of questionnaire was formulated to collect the responses from all the sample taken under consideration from the same competency parameters. All the three questionnaires have been attached in *Appendix I*, *Appendix II* and *Appendix III*.

3.8 Sampling Technique

The sampling technique is Purposive Sampling because top three ranking private banks were selected for the study (Axis, HDFC and ICICI Banks). Using Stratified Random Sampling, each state is further divided into 2 strata based on semi urban branch location. Using Purposive Sampling, 2 semi urban branches of each bank in each state were selected. Using Simple Random Sampling, 1 Branch Manager, 2 Assistant Manager (Operations), 2 Sales Manager and 1 Teller were selected for the study. The total employee from each semi urban branch is 5 and from each bank and each state is 10. Altogether 30 employees were selected from each state. The total number of sample, thus, taken for the study is 210.

Table 3.1 determined the sample unit and distribution of the respondents in the study area. An analysis results indicates that the selected state namely Meghalaya, Assam, Arunachal Pradesh, Manipur, Tripura, Mizoram and Nagaland contribute sample unit of 30 respondents taking 5 from each branch and altogether 10 respondents from each state and each branch from HDFC, Axis, and ICICI banks. Therefore the N number of respondents stands at 210 comprising all the 3 banks, and 70 from each bank respectively. The percentage of respondents stands at 14.29%.

Table 3.1: Location and Distribution of Respondents

STATE	AXIS BANK	No of Respon-dents	HDFC BANK	No of Respon-dents	ICICI BANK	No of Respon-dents	No of Respon-dents	Per-centage %
	Location (Semi urban branches)		Location (Semi urban branches)		Location(Semi urban branches)			
Meghalaya	Tura	5	Tura	5	Tura	5	30	14.29%
	Jowai	5	Jowai	5	Jowai	5		
Assam	Dhubri	5	Dhubri	5	Bongaigaon	5	30	14.29%
	Goalpara	5	Goalpara	5	Karimganj	5		
Arunachal Pradesh	Seppa	5	Hapoli	5	Itanagar	5	30	14.29%
	Naharlagun	5	Naharlagun	5	Naharlagun	5		
Manipur	Churachandpur	5	Churachandpur	5	Churachandpur	5	30	14.29%
	Moreh	5	Bishnupur	5	Porompat	5		
Mizoram	Kolasib	5	Champhai	5	Kolasib	5	30	14.29%
	Lunglei	5	Lunglei	5	Champhai	5		
Tripura	GB Bazar Branch	5	Jirania	5	Ambasa	5	30	14.29%
	Santir Bazar Branch	5	Dharmanagar	5	Santir Bazar	5		
Nagaland	Mokokchung	5	Mokokchung	5	Dimapur	5	30	14.29%
	Wokah	5	Wokah	5	Kohima	5		
Total	14	70	14	70	14	70	210	

Source: Computed from primary data.

3.9 Pilot Survey

A pilot study was done to validate the questionnaire. 50 employees were taken for this purpose. Cronbach's Alpha displays á = 0.65, meaning that 65% of the variability in a composite score is deemed appropriate, dependable, and would be improved by combining all 42 of the scale's items for objective 2 . Cronbach's alpha values á = 0.696 fell within the reliability scale's acceptable and suitable range for objective 3. The value derived is close to the maximum value of Cronbach's alpha of 1.00. This verifies whether the scale or data items are reliable and measures the same construct for the purpose of moving on to the next analytical stage. The table also displays á = 0.652, meaning that 65% of the variability in a composite score is deemed appropriate, dependable, and would be improved by combining all 210 of the scale's items. All the fuzzy and inappropriate questions have been deleted after the pilot survey and the questionnaire have been finalized.

3.10 Analytical Tools and Techniques

Statistical tests like Descriptive Statistics, Percentage, Relative Importance Index and ANOVA were used to derive a conclusion.

3.10.1 Descriptive Statistics

Descriptive Statistics summarizes, organizes and makes sense of the variability in data that have been gathered. The raw data results of the research have been represented through summary statistics. Descriptive statistics are important because they form the basis for further analysis. It demonstrates the relationship between variables in the given samples which is important for making inferential statistical comparisons. SPSS software have been used to provide the interpretations for descriptive statistics. (Nicholas, 2006; Kaur, Stoltfuz, and Yellapu,2018; Dong,2023; Kaushik and Mathur, 2014)

3.10.2 Frequency

The number of times an item repeats itself in the population is called frequency of that item. It reports the number of cases that fall into each category of the variable being analyzed.

3.10.3 Percentage

Percentage is a way of expressing a proportion as a fraction of 100. The total percentage of an entire dataset should always add up to 100%.

3.10.4 Valid Percent

Valid Percent is a percentage that does not include missing cases.

3.10.5 Cumulative Percent

Cumulative Percent adds the percentages of each region from the top of the table to the bottom culminating in 100%.

3.10.6 Mean

Mean is one of the measures of Central Tendency. Mean is the arithmetic average or the sum of values in a dataset divided by the quantities of observations. Mean is calculated only when the data is normally distributed and is strongly affected by outliers and skewed distributions. The formula for mean is:

Mean = (Sum of all observations/ Total number of observations)

3.10.7 Standard deviation

Standard Deviation was propounded by Karl Pearson denoted by sigma of Greek language. It is the square root of the arithmetic mean of the squares of deviations of the items from their mean value. In the words of Spiegel "The standard deviation is the square root of the arithmetic mean of the squares of all deviations. Deviations being measured from arithmetic mean of the items." The formula for standard deviation is:

$$\sigma = \sqrt{\frac{\Sigma(x_i - \mu)^2}{N}}$$

Where σ = population standard deviation

N = the size of population

x_i = each value from the population

μ = the population mean

3.11 Relative Importance Index

Kassem, Khoiry, and Hamzah, (2020) mentioned in their paper thatthe Relative Importance Index (RII) is used to describe the relative importance of the specific cause and effects based on the likelihood of occurrence and effect on the project using the Likert scale. Higher value of the index of Relative Importance (RII) is the critical cause or impact component and is determined by the equation:

$$\text{RII} = \frac{\Sigma W}{(A*N)}$$

Where,

RII= Relative Importance Index

W= Weight assigned to each factor by the respondents from 1 to 5 from strongly disagree, disagree, average, agree and very strongly agree.

A= is the highest weight

N= Total number of respondents

3.12 ANOVA

Turner and Thayer (2001) mentioned in their research that Analysis of Variance (ANOVA) is a statistical method developed by Ronald A. Fisher in his book "Statistical Methods for Research Workers" in 1920. This method is used to test differences between two or more population means. It is an extension of t-test that allow us to move beyond this in comparing the means of two population. ANOVA test is performed by comparing two types of variation, the variation between the sample means, as well as the variation within each of the samples. It is the most commonly used research method in business and economic literature. This is an important technique in determining the influence of some factors on other processing parameters.

Some of the assumptions of ANOVA are:

1. Each population is having normal distribution.
2. The population from which the samples are drawn have the equal variance. i.e $s_1^2 = s_2^2 = s_3^2 = s_4^2 \cdots\cdots = s_n^2$

3. Each sample is drawn randomly and they are independent.

$H_0: \mu_1 = \mu_2 = \mu_3 = \mu_4 .... = \mu_n$

$H_1: \mu_1 \neq \mu_2 \neq \mu_3 \neq \mu_4 .... \neq \mu_n$

3.12.1 One-way ANOVA

One-way ANOVA is one of the simplest cases which can be explained as one-way analysis of variance is used when the data are divided into groups according to only one factor.

Let us consider that the data $x_{11}, x_{12}, x_{13}, ..., x_{1m_1}$ are sample from population 1, $x_{21}, x_{22}, x_{23}, ... , x_{2n_2}$ are sample from population 2, ... ,$x_{k1}, x_{k2}, x_{k3}, ... , x_{kn_k}$ are sample from population k. Let x_{ij} denote the data from the ith group (level) and j^{th} observation.

We have values of independent normal variables X_{ij} ,$i = 1, 2, ... ,$ k and $j = 1, 2, ... , n_i$ with mean μ_i and constant standard deviation σ, $X_{ij} \sim N(\mu_i, \sigma)$. Alternatively, each $X_{ij} = \mu_i + \varepsilon_{ij}$ where ε_{ij} are normally distributed independent random errors, $\varepsilon_{ij} \sim N(0, \sigma)$. Let $N = n_1 + n_2 + \cdots + n_k$ is the total number of observations (the total sample size across all groups), where n_i is the sample size of the ith group.

The parameters of this models are the population means μ_1, $\mu_2, ..., \mu_k$ and the common standard deviation σ.

Using many separate two-sample *t*-tests to compare many pairs of means is a bad idea because we don't get a *p*-value or a confidence level for the complete set of comparisons together.

We will be interested in testing the null hypothesis

$$H_0 : \mu_1 = \mu_2 = \cdots = \mu_k \quad (1)$$

against the alternative hypothesis

$$H_1 : \exists 1 \leq i, \ l \leq k : \mu_i \neq \mu_l \quad (2)$$

(there is at least one pair with unequal means)

Let $\bar{x}_i$ represents the mean sample $i(i = 1, 2, ... , k)$:

$$\bar{x}_i = \frac{1}{n_i} \sum_{j=1}^{n_i} x_{ij} \quad (3)$$

$\bar{x}$ represents the grand mean, the mean of all the data points :

$$\bar{x} = \frac{1}{N}\sum_{i=1}^{k}\sum_{j=1}^{n_i} x_{ij} \tag{4}$$

s_i^2 represents the sample variance :

$$s_i^2 = \frac{1}{n_i - 1}\sum_{j=1}^{n_i}\left(x_{ij} - \bar{x}_i\right)^2 , \tag{5}$$

and $s^2 = MSE$ is an estimate of the variance σ^2 common to all k populations,

$$s^2 = \frac{1}{N - k}\sum_{i=1}^{k}(n_i - 1)\,.\,s_i^2 \tag{6}$$

ANOVA is centred around the idea to compare the variation between groups (levels) and the variation within samples by analyzing their variances.

Define the total sum of squares *SST*, sum of squares for error (or within groups) *SSE*, and the sum of squares for treatments (or between groups) *SSC*:

$$SST = \sum_{i=1}^{k}\sum_{j=1}^{n_i}\left(x_{ij} - \bar{x}\right)^2, \tag{7}$$

$$SSE = \sum_{i=1}^{k}\sum_{j=1}^{n_i}\left(x_{ij} - \bar{x}\right)^2 = \sum_{i=1}^{k}(n_i - 1).\,s_i^2, \tag{8}$$

$$SSC = \sum_{i=1}^{k}\sum_{j=1}^{n_i}(\bar{x}_i - \bar{x})^2 = \sum_{i=1}^{k} n_i\,.\,(\bar{x}_i - \bar{x})^2. \tag{9}$$

Let us consider the deviation from an observation to the grand mean written in the following way:

$$x_{ij} - \bar{x} = \left(x_{ij} - \bar{x}\right) + (\bar{x}_i - \bar{x}). \tag{10}$$

It is to be noticed that the left side is the heart of *SST*, and the right side has the analogous pieces of *SSE* and *SSC*. It actually works out that :

$$SST = SSE + SSC \tag{11}$$

The total mean sum of squares *MST*, the mean sums of squares for error *MSE*, and the mean sums of the squares for treatment *MS* Care :

$$MST = \frac{SST}{df(SST)} = \frac{SST}{N-1}, \quad (12)$$

$$MSE = \frac{SSE}{df(SSE)} = \frac{SSE}{N-k}, \quad (13)$$

$$MSC = \frac{SSC}{df(SSC)} = \frac{SSC}{k-1}. \quad (14)$$

The one-way ANOVA, assuming the test conditions are satisfied, uses the following statistic :

$$F = \frac{MSC}{MSE}. \quad (15)$$

Under H_0 the statistic has Fisher's distribution $F(k-1,\ N-k)$. In case it holds for the test criteria

$$F > F_{1-\alpha,\ k-1,\ N-k}, \quad (16)$$

Where $F_{1-\alpha,\ k-1,\ N-k}$ is $(1-\sigma)$ -quantile of *F*-distribution with $k-1$ and $N-k$ degrees of freedom, then hypothesis H_0 is rejected on significance level α[1,3].

The results of the computations that lead to the *F*-statistic are presented in an ANOVA table, the form of which is shown in table 3.2.

Table 3.2 Basic one-way ANOVA table

Variance source	Sum of squares SS	Degrees of freedom df	Mean square MS	F-statistic	Tail area above F
Between	*SSC*	$k-1$	*MSC*	*MSC/MSE*	*p*-value
Within	*SSE*	$N-k$	*MSE*	–	–
Total	*SST*	$N-1$	–	–	–

In Statistical softwaresthis is used to be in this column with *p*-value. This *p*-value says the probability of rejection the null hypothesis in case the null hypothesis holds. In case $p < \alpha$, where α is chosen significance level, is the null hypothesis rejected with probability greater than (1 - α). 100% probability. (Ostertagova and Ostertag, 2013)

References

Ostertagova, E. and Ostertag, O. (2013). Methodology and Application of One Way ANOVA. *American Journal of Mechanical Engineering, 1(7)*, 256-261.

Nicholas, J. (2006). Introduction to Descriptive Statistics. *Mathematics Learning Center*.

Kaur, P., Stoltfuz, J. and Yellapu, P. (2018). Descriptive Statistics. *International Journal of Academic Medicine. 4(1),* 60-63.

Dong, Y. (2023). Descriptive Statistics and its Application. *Highlights in Science, Engineering and Technology, 47,* 16-23.

Kaushik, M. and Mathur, B. (2014). Data Analysis of Students Marks with Descriptive Statistics. *International Journal on Recent and Innovation Trends in Computing and Communication*, *2*(5), 1188-1190.

Knapp, H. (2014). Introductory Statistics using SPSS. *Sage Publications, Inc.*

Turner, J.R. and Thayer, J. (2001). Introduction to Analysis of Variance. Design, Analysis and Interpretation. *Sage Publications, Inc.*

McCormick, Ernest J.; Jeanneret, Paul R.; Mecham, Robert C. (1969). The Development and Background of the Position Analysis Questionnaire (PAQ). *Occupational Research Center.*

Katz, R.L. (1955). Skills for an Effective Administrator. *Harvard Business Review.*

Goldberg, L.R. (1990). An Alternative Description of Personality: The Big Five Factor Structure, *Journal of Personality and Social Psychology*, *59*(6), 1216-29.

Cooley, C. H. (1902). *Human Nature and the Social Order*. Scribner.

Morey, D. *et al* (2001), *Knowledge Management*. Hyderabad: University Press.

Sheskin, D.J. (Ed.). (2007). Handbook of Parametric and Nonparametric Statistical Procedures. (4th Ed.). *Chapman and Hall/CRC*

White, R. (1959). Motivation reconsidered: The concept competence. *Psychological Review, 66*(5), 279–333

Kassem, M. A., Khoiry, M. A. and Hamzah, N. (2020). Using Relative Importance Index Method for Developing Risk Map in Oil and Gas Construction Projects. *Jurnal Kejuruteraan*, *32*(3), 85-97.

Chapter - 4

Analysis and Interpretations

4.1. Introduction

This chapter mainly strive to analyze and understand the analysis on job description, employee competency level as desired by the branch managers, and overall employee score on the parameters of the Iceberg Model: knowledge, skills, self-concept, traits and motives, with a score from 5 to 1, where 5 indicates most competent and 1 indicates least competent. To serve the objectives of the study, stepwise analyses such as frequency distribution, mean, standard deviation, percentage, and ANOVA analysis were conducted.

SECTION - 1

The analysis in this section is based on the components of PAQ Questionnaire (*Jeanneret and Mecham ,1969)*. The responses have been classified on the basis of the following parameters, Information input, Mental Processes, Work output, Relationship with other persons, Job context and Job related variables.

4.1.1 Information Input

Table 4.1. Age of the Respondents

Age	Frequency	Percent	Valid Percent	Cumulative Percent
21-35	95	45.2	45.2	12.3
36-50	89	42.6	42.6	87.7
51>Above	26	12.3	12.3	100
Total	**210**	**100**	**100**	

Source: Computed from primary data.

Table 4.1 highlights the different age groups of the private bank employees of 3 select banks in North-East India. The study found that 45.2 % of the employees falls under the age group of 21-35 years followed by 42.6% under the age group of 36-50 years. An intensive study is being conducted to understand and evaluate the demographic characteristics of the bank employees in the sample unit.

For conducting a study on the comparison of the mean of the various independent variables on several occasions, such as gender, the respondents are categorically segregated into two genders, such as male and female. The analysis result of the study is presented herewith as follows:

Table 4.2: Gender of Respondents

Gender	Frequency	Percent	Valid Percent	Cumulative Percent
Male	84	40	40	40
Female	126	60	60	100
Total	**210**	**100**	**100**	

Source: Computed from primary data

Table 4.2 shows gender participation as an employee of various private banks in north-east India, and it is found that 126 respondents, consisting of 60 percent of the total sample unit, belong to a female category, and the remaining 84 respondents, with 40 percent of the total employees, belong to a male category.

Table 4.3 Marital Status of Respondents

Marital Status	Frequency	Percent	Valid Percent	Cumulative Percent
Unmarried	23	10.5	10.5	10.5
Married	181	86.5	86.5	97.0
Divorce/ Separated, Widow	6	3.03	3.03	100
Total	**210**	**100**	**100**	

Source: computed from primary data

Table 4.3 endeavors to showcase the marital status of respondents in the study area. It was found that 181 respondents, consisting of

86.5 percent of bank employees, are married, and 23 respondents, or 10.5 percent of the sample unit are unmarried. The remaining 12 respondents, or 3.03 percent of the total employees, fall under the category of divorced, separated, or widowed.

Descriptive Statistics of Selected Variables

In this section, an attempt was made to analysis and understand the basic characteristics of the respondents. The primary data was collected from the selected private banks employees of north east India and step-wise analysis of the variables are presented as follows:

Table 4.4 Descriptive Statistics of Selected Variables

Variables	N	Mini-mum	Maxi-mum	Mean (μ)	S.D (σ)
Level of Management	210	1	3	3	0.207
Year of service in present organization	210	1	15	3.60	1.881
Job category	210	1	3	3	1.210
Awareness of job analysis	210	1	5	4	0.610
Awareness of job description	210	1	5	3.17	0.696
Knowledge of job specific	210	1	5	4.11	0.728
Importance of job analysis	210	1	5	3.98	0.320

Source: Computed from Primary data

Table 4.4 determines the descriptive statistics of the selected variable to understand the basic characteristics of the respondents. An investigation reveals that the mean value on the level of management was found at the 3 levels of categories, which highlights that the majority of the managerial respondents are at the lower level of management, having 3 to 4 years of service in the present organization. With reference to respondents' awareness of job analysis, the study shows that the majority of the respondents fall under the construct scale of 4, meaning that respondents are aware of job analysis, followed by job description awareness, which exhibits a scale of 3.17 in the range of neutral to awareness level. The study shows the respondent knowledge of job-specificity at 4.11 construct level, which is the category of aware to strongly aware. Importance of job analysis exhibits a construct scale of 3.98 in the range of important level.

4.1.2 Mental Processes

Frequency, Mean, Standard Deviation, and Percentage

An attempt was made to identify and understand the overall analysis of three banks, such as Axis, HDFC, and ICICI, on the job description analysis of private banks in North East India. The descriptive statistics, such as frequency range, mean, standard deviation, and percentage, were systematically analyzed and presented into three (3) smaller tables as follows:

NAC- Not at at Important, NI - Not Important, I - Important, VI - very important

Table 4.5 showcases the mean value, standard deviation, frequency, percentage, and level of agreement on the overall job analysis conducted by banks in identifying the job description in the study area. The analysis result showcases the agreement variables of 10 items, and the construct-level impact was from a point scale of not at all important to very important. The study indicates the job description agreement level of 7 items was found to be important in taking up the responsibility of employees, namely, item #1 (μ= 1.87, σ= 0.081) 'offer appropriate finance services', item # 3 (μ= 3.80, σ= 0.421)'selling ability', item #4 (μ = 2.94, σ= 0.451)'managing cash and gold loans', item #5 (μ= 2.50, σ= 0.681)'monitoring NPA', item #6 (μ= 2.35, σ= 0.794)'managing customers', item #7 (μ= 1.65, σ = 0.982) ' Back-end tasks like verifying information, data entry, cross-verifying transaction information', item #8 (μ= 2.08, σ= 0.489)'Financial data management'.

An analysis further showcases the overall job analysis on job descriptions of various private banks. It is found that the agreement level of 2 variables is average; the description is shown in items #9 (μ = 3.86, σ= 0.081) 'organization skills', and item #10 (μ= 3.95, σ= 0.084) 'automatic services'. There is only one parameter that indicates a very importantjob description, such as item #2 (μ= 2.03, σ= 0.432), 'bringing new business'.

Table 4.5: Overall Banks Analysis on Job Description of Private Bank on Selected Variables (A)

Sl	Variables	M (μ)	S. D (σ)	NAI (%)	NI (%)	A (%)	I (%)	VI (%)	Level
1.	Offer appropriate finance services	1.87	0.081	0	12 (5.7)	33 (15.6)	111 (52.4)	54 (25.5)	Important
2.	Bringing new business	2.03	0.432	0	0	1(0.5)	52(24.5)	157(74.1)	Very Important
3.	Selling ability	3.80	0.421	0	48(17)	17(6)	142(50.4)	3(1.1)	Important
4.	Managing cash and gold loan	2.94	0.451	0	56(19.9)	8(2.8)	146(51.8)	0	Important
5.	Monitoring NPA	3.50	0.681	0	54(19.1)	8(2.8)	143(50.7)	5(1.8)	Important
6.	Managing customers	2.35	0.794	0	0	12(5.7)	197(93.8)	1(0.4)	Important
7.	Back-end task like verifying information, data entry, cross-verifying transaction information	1.65	0.982	0	10(3.5)	7(2.5)	193(68.)	72(25.5)	Important
8.	Financial data management	2.08	0.489	0	11(3.9)	4(1.4)	180(91.1)	15(4.6)	Important
9.	Organization skills	3.86	0.081	0	15 (4.6)	165(84.6)	20(8.9)	10(2.6)	Average
10.	Automation services	3.95	0.084	0	10(3.2)	177(88.9)	15(4.6)	8(2.8)	Average

Source: Computed from primary data

Table 4.6: Overall Banks Analysis on Job Description of Private Bank on Selected Variables (B)

Sl	Variables	M (μ)	S. D (σ)	HS (%)	TS (%)	CS (%)	Level
1.	Skills require on offer appropriate financial services to the branch	2.98	0.672	27(9.6)	16(5.7)	167(84.7)	Conceptual Skill
2.	Managing customer requirements	2.85	0.002	171(86.1)	1(0.4)	38(13.5)	Human skills
3.	Selling ability	3.86	0.411	190(92.9)	0	20(7.1)	Human skills
4.	Managing cash and gold loan	2.19	0.433	181(89.7)	19(7.3)	10(3.2)	Human skills
5.	Monitoring NPA	3.56	0.981	185(91)	10(3.2)	15(4.7)	Human skills
6.	Back-end task like verifying information, data entry, cross-verifying transaction information	1.89	0.897	150(77.7)	45(16)	15(5.3)	Human skills
7.	Financial data management	3.09	.0678	9(3.2)	156(80.8)	45(16)	Technical skills
8.	Organization skills	3.98	0.983	111(64.9)	48(17)	51(18.1)	Human skills
9.	Automation services	1.96	0.649	12(4.3)	193(91.9)	5(2.4)	Technical skills

Source: Computed from primary data

HS- Human Skills, TS- technical Skills, CS- Conceptual Skills

Table 4.6 highlights the mean value, standard deviation, frequency, percentage, and overall job analysis conducted by banks in identifying the job description based on skills in the study area. The analysis result determined the analysis of nine job description variables, and the construct was based on variables such as technical skills, human skills, and conceptual skills. The study indicates the job description agreement level of 6 items was found to be important in taking up the human skills, namely, item #2 ($\mu = 2.85, \sigma = 0.002$)'managing customer requirements', item #3 ($\mu = 3.86$, $\sigma = 0.411$)'selling ability', item #4 ($\mu=2.19, \sigma=0.433$)'managing cash and gold loan', item #5()'monitoring NPA', item #6 ($\mu = 3.56$, $\sigma = 0.981$) 'back-end task like verifying information, data entry, cross-verifying transaction information', and item #8 ($\mu = 3.98$, $\sigma = 0.983$) 'organization'. The study reveals that each job description was conceptual skills, namely item #1 ($\mu = 2.98$, $\sigma = 0.671$),'skills 'required to offer appropriate financial services to the branch', and item #9 ($\mu = 1.96, \sigma = 0.649$), 'automation services', which were considered technical skills in the study area.

Table 4.7: Mental Demands for the job

The mental demands that are required in the job in terms of the level of concentration and the duration of mental effort	Frequency	Percentage (%)
Intermittent	-	-
Normal	167	79.5
Continual	43	20.4
Total	**210**	**100**

Table 4.7 states that the mental demand as interpreted through the responses states that 167 respondents (79.5%) responded the mental demand to be normal and 43 (20.4%) respondents claimed to be continual.

4.1.3 Work Output

- 100% of the respondents responded that audible and visual demands are required for the job.
- AXIS and ICICI Banks use PINACLE Software and HDFC Bank use ORACLE software.

- 84% claimed that the level of proficiency for using the technical knowledge is advanced and 16% claimed to be intermediate.

4.1.4 Relationship With Other Persons

Table 4.8: Overall Banks Analysis on Job Description of Private Bank on Selected Variables (C)

Sl	Variables	M (µ)	S. D (σ)	S.D.A (%)	DA (%)	N (%)	A	SA	Level
1.	The incumbent is require to have a high level of contact with staff or customers	3.80	0.421	0	7 (1.1)	93 (33)	110 (66.7)	0	Agree
2.	The incumbent often works as part of a team	2.94	0.451	0	9 (1.5)	75 (26.6)	125 (72.6)	0	Agree
3.	The incumbents is responsible for the work of others	3.50	0.681	0	5 (1)	10 (3.6)	85 (31.9)	110 (65)	Strongly agree
4.	The incumbent is often place in conflict situations with customers or staff member where people may be angry or rude during these times	3.68	0.362	0	23 (8.2)	24 (8.5)	88 (56.6)	75 (26.6)	Agree

SDA- Strongly Disagree, DA- Disagree, N-Neutral, A - Agree, SA- Strongly agree

Table 4.8 determines the mean value, standard deviation, frequency, percentage, and overall job analysis conducted by banks in identifying the relationship the employees share with others based on selected variables in the study area. The analysis result exhibits an analysis of job description variables of 4 items, and the agreement was from a level of strongly disagree to strongly agree. The study indicates the job description agreement level of 3 items was found to agree level on the analysis of job description, namely item #1 (µ = 3.80, σ = 0.421) 'The incumbent is require to have a high level of contact with staff or customers', item #2 (μ = 2.94, σ = 0.451) 'the incumbent often works as part of a team', item #4 (μ = 3.68, σ = 0.362) 'the incumbent is often place in conflict situations with customers or staff member where people may be angry or rude during these times' and 1 item is found to be on strongly agree level #3(μ=3.50, σ =0.681) 'The incumbents is responsible for the work of others'.

Table 4.9: Relative Importance Index (RII) Ranking on Importance of Job description of Private Banks (B)

Sl	Variables	S.D.A	DA	N	A	SA	Total Number	A*N	RII	Rank
1.	The incumbent is require to have a high level of contact with staff or customers	0	28	279	220	0	527	1050	0.50	1
2.	The incumbent often works as part of a team	0	36	225	250	0	511	1050	0.49	2
3.	The incumbents is responsible for the work of others	0	20	30	170	110	330	1050	0.31	4
4.	The incumbent is often place in conflict situations with customers or staff member where people may be angry or rude during these times	0	92	72	176	75	415	1050	0.39	3

SDA- Strongly Disagree, DA- Disagree, N-Neutral, A - Agree, SA- Strongly agree

Table 4.9 determines the Relative Importance Index (RII) along with the appropriate importance level and ranking. The following rating criteria were adopted on a 5-point Likert scale according to level of significance. #1 'The incumbent is require to have a high level of contact with staff or customers' is ranked 1st with RII of 0.50, followed by #2 'The incumbent often works as part of a team' with RII of 0.49 ranks 2nd, #4 'The incumbent is often place in conflict situations with customers or staff member where people may be angry or rude during these times' with RII of 0.39 stands at 3rd Rank and #3 'The incumbents is responsible for the work of others' with RII of 0.31 stands at 4th Rank.

4.1.5 Job Context

Table 4.10 Level of responsibility the incumbent takes for damage caused

Sl	Variables	M (μ)	S. D (σ)	Never (%)	Rarely (%)	Some-time (%)	Often (%)	Always (%)	Level
1.	Responsibility for damage	2.88	0.946	9 (1.5)	30 (10.3)	31 (11)	67 (23)	82 (52)	Always

Table 5.10 depicts the level of responsibility the incumbent takes for waste, damage, defects or other loss of value to material assets (e.g., parts, equipment, or cash) caused by inadequate job performance or inattentiveness. The level is found highest at the construct of 'always' with 82 respondents and 52 %

4.1.6 Job Related Variables

Table 4.11 Level of Supervision received by the incumbent

Sl	Variables	M (μ)	S. D (σ)	Never (%)	Rarely (%)	Some-time (%)	Often (%)	Always (%)	Level
1.	Level of Supervision received	1.72	1.67	0	0	21 (10.0)	87 (41.7)	102 (48.3)	Always

Table 4.11 depicts the level of supervision received by the employees and 102 respondents with 48.3% leveled that they always receive supervision by the supervisors.

SECTION - 2

4.2 Importance of Employees Competency Level Appraised by Manager

An analysis is performed to highlight the competency level of the manager evaluated the managers of each selected bank. The stepwise analysis is run to identify and understand their frequencies and the significance difference in the mean score among the selected private banks.

Table 4.12: Reliability Test

Cronbach's Alpha	Cronbach's Alpha Based on standardized items	N of items
0.726	0.658	42

Source: Collected from Primary Data

Table 4.12 highlights the variables' Cronbach's alpha values ά = 0.726, falling within the reliability scale's acceptable and adequate range. Additionally, the value derived from the 20 items is in close proximity to the maximum value of Cronbach's alpha, which is 1.00. This verifies whether the scale or data items are reliable and measures the same construct for the purpose of moving on to the next analytical stage.

The table also displays ά = 0.65, meaning that 65% of the variability in a composite score is deemed appropriate, dependable, and would be improved by combining all 42 of the scale's items.

Table 4.13 highlights the level of importance assigned to each of the parameters by the Branch managers. Item #3 'knowledge in products and services (μ= 4.34, σ =0.540), item #6 'knowledge in relationship' (μ= 4.41, σ =0.631), item #7 'technical skills' (μ= 4.02, σ =0.419), item #34 'responsibility' (μ= 3.92, σ =0.480) are found to be very important by the Branch Managers.

Item #1 'customer knowledge' (μ= 4.14, σ =0.482), item #2 'knowledge in people' (μ= 3.46, σ =0.789), item# 4 'knowledge in process' (μ= 3.90, σ =0.435), item #15 'emotional stability' (μ= 3.71, σ =1.325) item#16 'extroversion'(μ= 4.12, σ =0.561) item#17 'introversion'(μ= 3.45, σ =0.670)item#18 'openness to experience'(μ= 4.19, σ =0.204), item #20 'technical supervision (μ=3.19,σ=0.890) item#21interpersonal relationship with supervisors (μ= 2.70, σ =0.682), item#23 'interpersonal relationship with subordinates' (μ=3.02, σ=2.431)item #28 'status' (μ=3.09, σ=0.59), item #29 'achievement' (μ= 3.56, σ =0.984) item#33'possibility of growth' (μ= 4.08, σ =0.386) are considered to be important by the branch managers.

Table 4.13: Mean, S.D., Frequency, Percentage, and Level of Competency Appraised by Manager

Sl.	Reasons	M (μ)	S. D (σ)	NAI (%)	NI (%)	A (%)	I (%)	VI (%)	Level
1.	Customer knowledge	4.14	0.482	0	0	13	24	5	Important
2.	Knowledge in people	3.46	0.789	0	2	12	28	0	Important
3.	Knowledge in products and services	4.34	0.540	0	0	1	4	37	Very Important
4.	Knowledge in process	3.90	0.435	0	0	3	32	7	Important
5.	Organizational memory	2.84	0.552	0	12	23	7	0	Average
6.	Knowledge in relationship	4.41	0.631	0	0	2	18	22	Very Important
7.	Technical skills	4.02	0.419	0	3	11	13	15	Very Important
8.	Human skills	4.02	0.294	0	2	10	18	12	Important
9.	Conceptual skills	3.42	0.649	0	0	9	32	1	Important
10.	The imagination of our appearance to the other person (what employees feel about you)	3.12	0.493	0	3	27	9	4	Average
11.	The imagination of his judgment of that appearance (how do you react to what other employees feel about you)	2.30	0.611	0	4	17	12	9	Average
12.	Some sort of self-feeling such as pride or mortification	3.86	0.872	0	0	28	11	3	Average
13.	Agreeableness	3.19	0.594	0	6.7	50.0	41.7	1.7	Average
14.	Conscientiousness	3.08	1.105	6	14	12	8	2	Not Important
15.	Emotional stability	3.71	1.325	1	3	5	17	6	Important
16.	Extroversion	4.12	0.561	2	1	8	17	14	Important
17.	Introversion	3.45	0.670	0	5	35	43.3	16.7	Important

18.	Openness to experience	4.19	0.204	0	0	0	27	15	Important
19.	Company policy and administration	2.92	1.103	0	0	23	17	2	Average
20.	Technical supervision	3.19	0.890	0	20	18.3	50.0	11.7	Important
21.	Interpersonal relationship with supervisors	2.70	0.682	0	0	11	27	4	Important
22.	Interpersonal relationship with peers	3.67	1.100	0	0	3	19	20	Very Important
23.	Interpersonal relationship with subordinates	3.02	2.431	0	0	12	17	13	Important
24.	Salary	2.61	0.896	0	23	9	8	2	Not adequate
25.	Job security	3.58	1.089	0	12	19	6	5	Average
26.	Personal life	3.06	0.965	0	8	14	10	10	Average
27.	Working conditions	3.23	0.929	0	9	16	15	2	Average
28.	Status	3.09	0.59	0	4	6	19	13	Important
29.	Achievement	3.56	0.984	0	4	10	20	8	Important
30.	Recognition	3.03	0.598	10	12	18	2	0	Average
31.	Advancement	4.04	0.545	0	4	19	9	10	Average
32.	Work itself	4.60	0.502	3	11	14	10	4	Average
33.	Possibility of growth	4.08	0.386	0	8	13	14	7	Important
34.	Responsibility	3.92	0.480	0	3	8	15	16	Very Important

Sources: Computed from the primary data

Note: NAI= Not at all Important, NI= NotImportant, A = Average, I= Important, VI = Very Important

S. D = Standard Deviation, M = Mean

Item #14 'conscientiousness' (μ= 3.08, σ =1.105) is considered to be not important item #24 'salary' (μ= 2.61, σ =0.896) is found not to be adequate by the branch managers.

Item #5 'organizational memory' (μ= 2.84, σ =0.552), item #10 'The imagination of our appearance to the other person'(μ= 3.12, σ =0.493) item #11' The imagination of his judgment of that appearance'(μ= 2.60, σ =0.611) item #12 'Some sort of self-feeling such as pride or mortification'(μ= 3.86, σ =0.872) item#13 'Agreeableness'(μ= 3.19, σ =0.594)item#19 'company policy and administration'(μ= 2.92, σ =1.103) item#25'job security'(μ= 3.58, σ =1.089) item#26'personal life'(μ= 3.06, σ =0.965) item#27'working conditions'(μ= 3.23, σ =0.929) item#30 'recognition'(μ= 3.03, σ =0.598) item#31'advancement'(μ= 4.04, σ =0.545) item#32'work itself'(μ= 4.60, σ =0.502) are considered to be of average importance by the branch managers.

4.3 ANOVA Analysis

This section is an attempt to measure the variance of the population's different scores. The bank employees mean score differences were evaluated by the manager level based on factors such as knowledge, skills, self-concept, and traits. The results of the one-way analysis of variance are herewith as follows:

Table 4.14: Significance of Difference in Mean Score on the Parameter of Knowledge appraised by the Branch Managers

ANOVA						
		Sum of Squares	df	Mean Square	F	Sig.
Customer knowledge	Between Groups	8.190	2	4.095	8.908	.001
	Within Groups	17.929	39	.460		
	Total	26.119	41			
Knowledge in people	Between Groups	4.333	2	2.167	1.571	.221
	Within Groups	53.786	39	1.379		
	Total	58.119	41			
Knowledge in products and services	Between Groups	2.286	2	1.143	2.137	.132
	Within Groups	20.857	39	.535		
	Total	23.143	41			

Knowledge in process	Between Groups	.143	2	.071	.269	.766
	Within Groups	10.357	39	.266		
	Total	10.500	41			
Organi-sational memory	Between Groups	.619	2	.310	.949	.396
	Within Groups	12.714	39	.326		
	Total	13.333	41			
Knowledge in relationship	Between Groups	1.000	2	.500	1.542	.227
	Within Groups	12.643	39	.324		
	Total	13.643	41			

Source: Primary Data

Table 4.14 determined that the competency level of employees across the select private banks as desired by the bank managers on the parameters of knowledge across 3 banks, namely Axis, HDFC and ICICI Banks Ltd. The results interpret that there is a significant difference between the variable based on 'customer knowledge' (F= 8.908, p=0.001) at the 5% level. An investigation further shows that the mean score of HDFC Bank(μ= 3.64) is the highest followed by mean scores of ICICI Bank (μ=3.50) and Axis Bank(μ= 2.64) which means that the branch managers of HDFC Banks considers the variable 'customer knowledge' to be most important followed by ICICI and Axis Bank. For the variables 'knowledge in people' (F=1.571, p=.221), 'knowledge in products and services' (F=2.137, p=.132), 'knowledge in process' (F=.269, p= .766), 'organizational memory' (F=.949, p=.396), 'knowledge in relationship' (F= 1.542, p=.227) means there is no significant difference amongst the banks in terms of importance given by the branch managers meaning the managers give equal importance to the knowledge competency parameters mentioned above.

Table 4.15: Significance of Difference in Mean Score on the Parameter of Skills appraised by the Branch Managers

ANOVA						
		Sum of Squares	df	Mean Square	F	Sig.
Technical skills	Between Groups	.333	2	.167	.752	.478
	Within Groups	8.643	39	.222		
	Total	8.976	41			
Human skills	Between Groups	.190	2	.095	.261	.771
	Within Groups	14.214	39	.364		
	Total	14.405	41			
Conceptual skills	Between Groups	2.905	2	1.452	2.403	.104
	Within Groups	23.571	39	.604		
	Total	26.476	41			

In table 4.15, variables such as technical skills (F= .752, p= .478), human skills (F= .261, p= .771) and conceptual skills (F=2.403, p= .104) it is observed that the null hypothesis is accepted, and there is no significant difference between the competency parameters at 5% level of significance which means the managers from all the 3 banks give equal importance to all the skills in this competency parameter.

Table 4.16: Significance of Difference in Mean Score on the Parameter of Self Concept appraised by the Branch Managers

ANOVA						
		Sum of Squares	df	Mean Square	F	Sig.
The imagination of our appearance to the other person (what employees feel about you)	Between Groups	3.000	2	1.500	1.400	.259
	Within Groups	41.786	39	1.071		
	Total	44.786	41			
The imagination of his judgment of that appearance (how do you react to what other employees feel about you)	Between Groups	.333	2	.167	.576	.567
	Within Groups	11.286	39	.289		
	Total	11.619	41			

Some sort of self-feeling such as pride or mortification	Between Groups	1.476	2	.738	1.857	.170
	Within Groups	15.500	39	.397		
	Total	16.976	41			

In table 4.16, variables such as 'the imagination of our appearance to the other person' (F= 1.40, p= .259), 'the imagination of his judgment of that appearance' (F= .576, p= .567) and 'some sort of self-feeling such as pride or mortification' (F= 1.857, p= .170) it is observed that the null hypothesis is accepted, and there is no significant difference between the competency parameters at 5% level of significance which means the managers from all the 3 banks give equal importance to all the self-concept variables in this competency parameter.

Table 4.17: Significance of Difference in Mean Score on the Parameter of Traits appraised by the Branch Managers

ANOVA						
		Sum of Squares	df	Mean Square	F	Sig.
Agreeableness	Between Groups	5.190	2	2.595	10.900	.000
	Within Groups	9.286	39	.238		
	Total	14.476	41			
Conscientious-ness	Between Groups	1.333	2	.667	1.384	.263
	Within Groups	18.786	39	.482		
	Total	20.119	41			
Emotional stability	Between Groups	.619	2	.310	.383	.684
	Within Groups	31.500	39	.808		
	Total	32.119	41			
Extroversion	Between Groups	.048	2	.024	.027	.973
	Within Groups	33.857	39	.868		
	Total	33.905	41			
Introversion	Between Groups	1.476	2	.738	1.700	.196
	Within Groups	16.929	39	.434		
	Total	18.405	41			
Openness to experience	Between Groups	8.714	2	4.357	11.383	.000
	Within Groups	14.929	39	.383		
	Total	23.643	41			

In table 5.17, variables such as 'Conscientiousness' (F= 1.384, p= .263), 'Emotional stability' (F= .383, p= .684) and 'extroversion' (F= .027, p= .973), introversion (F= 1.7,p= .196) it is observed that the null hypothesis is accepted, and there is no significant difference between the competency parameters at 5% level of significance which means the managers from all the 3 banks give equal importance to all thesetrait variables in this competency parameter.

For the variable 'agreeableness' (F= 10.9, p= .000), there is a significant level of difference at 5% level between the preferred competency level of various banks in North East India. A further comparison in the mean scores of the 3 banks indicate that HDFC Bank has the highest mean (μ= 3.64) followed by Axis Bank (μ=3.14) and ICICI Bank (μ= 2.79). The Branch Managers of HDFC Bank give more preference to this competency parameter followed by Axis and ICICI bank branch managers.

For the variable 'openness to experience' (F=11.383, p=.000), there is a significant level of difference between the preferred competency level of various banks in North East India. A further comparison in the mean scores of the 3 banks indicate that ICICI Bank has the highest mean (μ= 4.00) followed by Axis Bank (μ=3.07) and HDFC Bank (μ= 3.00). The Branch Managers of ICICI Bank give more preference to this competency parameter followed by Axis and HDFC bank branch managers.

Table 4.18: Significance of Difference in Mean Score on the Parameter of Motives appraised by the Branch Managers

ANOVA						
		Sum of Squares	df	Mean Square	F	Sig.
Company policy and administration	Between Groups	.190	2	.095	.213	.809
	Within Groups	17.429	39	.447		
	Total	17.619	41			
Technical supervision	Between Groups	7.762	2	3.881	6.124	.005
	Within Groups	24.714	39	.634		
	Total	32.476	41			
Interpersonal relationship with supervisors	Between Groups	15.429	2	7.714	21.937	.000
	Within Groups	13.714	39	.352		
	Total	29.143	41			

Interpersonal relationship with peers	Between Groups	2.048	2	1.024	1.291	.286
	Within Groups	30.929	39	.793		
	Total	32.976	41			
Interpersonal relationship with subordinates	Between Groups	.143	2	.071	.214	.808
	Within Groups	13.000	39	.333		
	Total	13.143	41			
Salary	Between Groups	4.619	2	2.310	4.029	.026
	Within Groups	22.357	39	.573		
	Total	26.976	41			
Job security	Between Groups	16.714	2	8.357	10.838	.000
	Within Groups	30.071	39	.771		
	Total	46.786	41			
Personal life	Between Groups	7.762	2	3.881	6.269	.004
	Within Groups	24.143	39	.619		
	Total	31.905	41			
Working conditions	Between Groups	3.000	2	1.500	4.627	.016
	Within Groups	12.643	39	.324		
	Total	15.643	41			
Status	Between Groups	1.476	2	.738	.745	.481
	Within Groups	38.643	39	.991		
	Total	40.119	41			
Achievement	Between Groups	2.048	2	1.024	1.827	.174
	Within Groups	21.857	39	.560		
	Total	23.905	41			
Recognition	Between Groups	3.190	2	1.595	1.792	.180
	Within Groups	34.714	39	.890		
	Total	37.905	41			
Advancement	Between Groups	2.286	2	1.143	1.371	.266
	Within Groups	32.500	39	.833		
	Total	34.786	41			
Work itself	Between Groups	2.048	2	1.024	1.160	.324
	Within Groups	34.429	39	.883		
	Total	36.476	41			
Possibility of growth	Between Groups	.333	2	.167	.892	.418
	Within Groups	7.286	39	.187		
	Total	7.619	41			

Responsibility	Between Groups	4.905	2	2.452	3.514	.040
	Within Groups	27.214	39	.698		
	Total	32.119	41			

Sources: Primary data

In table 4.18, the variable 'technical supervision' (F=6.124, p=.005) means we are rejecting the null hypothesis and there is a significant difference at 5% level between the responses of the branch managers of the given banks under consideration. The study determined the branch managers of ICICI Bank (μ=3.79) has the highest mean score followed by HDFC (μ=3.00) and Axis Bank (μ=2.79), indicating the highest mean with the highest preference in the variable of technical supervision.

The variable 'interpersonal relationship with supervisors' (F= 21.937, p=.000) there are significant differences at 5% level between the responses by the branch managers with regard to this variable. A further investigation shows that ICICI Bank has the highest mean score (μ=4.00) exhibiting higher preference for this competency parameter followed by equal mean scores (μ=2.71) for both Axis and HDFC Banks indicating the same level of preference.

The variable 'Salary' (F= 21.937, p=.000) there are significant differences at 5% level between the responses by the branch managers with regard to this variable. A further investigation shows that ICICI Bank has the highest mean score (μ=4.00) exhibiting higher preference for this competency parameter followed by equal mean scores (μ=2.71) for both Axis and HDFC Banks indicating the same level of preference.

The variable 'Job Security' (F= 10.838, p=.000) there are significant differences at 5% level between the responses by the branch managers. A further investigation shows that ICICI Bank has the highest mean score (μ=3.57) exhibiting higher preference for this competency parameter followed by mean scores of (μ=3.14) for HDFC Bank and the lowest mean score of (μ=2.07) for Axis Bank. The responses further indicate that ICICI Branch Managers feel mostly that there is less job security followed by HDFC and Axis Banks.

The variable 'Personal life' (F=6.269, p=.004) is found to be significant at 5% level. A comparison in the mean scores (μ= 2.57) ICICI Bank, (μ=2.86), HDFC Bank and (μ=2.64) Axis Bank indicates that the Branch Managers of ICICI Bank give more importance to personal life followed by HDFC and ICICI Bank.

The variable 'working condition' (F=4.627, p=.016) is found to be significant at 5% level. The mean scores of (μ=2.71), for ICICI Bank followed by mean score of (μ=2.29) for HDFC Bank and (μ= 2.07) for Axis Bank indicates that the managers of ICICI Bank give more importance to working conditions followed by HDFC and Axis Bank.

The variable 'responsibility' (F=3.514, p=.040) is found to be significant at 5% level. This implies that Axis Bank managers give more importance to responsibility (μ=3.71) followed by managers of ICICI Bank (μ=2.57) and HDFC Bank (μ=2.43).

The variables 'company policy and administration' (F=.213, p=.809), 'interpersonal relationship with peers' (F=1.291, p=.286), 'interpersonal relationship with subordinates' (F=.214, p=.808), 'status' (F=.745, p=.481), 'achievement' (F=1.827, p=.174) 'recognition' (F=1.792, p=.180) 'advancement'(F=1.371, p=.266) 'work itself' (F=1.160, p=.324) 'possibility of growth' (F=.892, p=.418) shows no significant difference at 5% level which means the branch managers give equal importance to all the above mentioned variables.

SECTION - 3

4.4 Reliability Test

To verify the reliability of the collected data, reliability statistics were conducted. There are altogether 210 samples to accommodate the analysis, confirming the data appropriateness with a suitable score for the reliability test.

Table 4.19: Reliability Statistics

Overall Employees competency Level in Cronbach's Alpha		
Cronbach's Alpha	**Cronbach's Alpha Based on Standardized Items**	**No. of items**
0.696	0.652	210

Sources: Primary data

Table 4.19 determined that the Cronbach's alpha values ά = 0.696 fell within the reliability scale's acceptable and suitable range. The value derived is close to the maximum value of Cronbach's alpha of 1.00. This verifies whether the scale or data items are reliable and measures the same construct for the purpose of moving on to the next analytical stage. The table also displays ά = 0.652, meaning that 65% of the variability in a composite score is deemed appropriate, dependable, and would be improved by combining all 210 of the scale's items.

Table 4.20: Overall Banks Employees Competency Based on Knowledge Factor

Sl	Competency	M (μ)	S. D (σ)	NAC (%)	NC (%)	A (%)	C (%)	VC (%)	Level
1.	Customer knowledge	4.01	0.460	0	1(0.5)	18 (8.5)	168 (79.2)	23 (10.8)	Com-petent
2.	Knowledge in people	3.99	0.800	0	12 (5.7)	33 (15.6)	111 (52.4)	54 (25.5)	Com-petent
3.	Knowledge in products and services	4.74	0.449	0	0	1 (0.5)	52 (24.5)	157 (74.1)	Very com-petent
4.	Knowledge in process	3.80	0.421	0	0	33 (15.6)	169 (79.7)	8 (3.8)	Com-petent
5.	Organizational memory	2.94	0.451	0	28 (13.2)	166 (78.3)	16 (7.5)	0	Average
6.	Knowledge in relationship	4.50	0.681	0	0	9 (4.2)	88 (41.5)	113 (53.3)	Very com-petent

Sources: Computed from primary data

NAV = Not at all Competent, NC = Not Competent, N = Neutral, C = Competent, and HC = Highly Competent

Table 4.20 showcases the mean value, standard deviation, frequency, percentage, and level of agreement on overall employee competency in the study area. The analysis result showcases the agreement variables of six items, and the construct-level impact was from a point scale of not at all competent to very competent. The study indicates the agreement level of 2 items was found to be very competent based on the KSA score parameter in taking up the role responsibility of employees, namely, item #3 ($\mu = 4.741, \sigma = 0.449$). 'knowledge in products and services', and item # 6 ($\mu = 4.50, \sigma = 0.681$), 'knowledge in relationships'. An investigation result indicates that of the total variables, three (3) items are found to be competent, such as item #1 ($\mu = 4.10, \sigma = 0.460$), 'customer knowledge', item #2 ($\mu = 3.99, \sigma = 0.800$), 'knowledge in people', and item #4 ($\mu = 3.80, \sigma = 0.421$), 'knowledge in process'. Finally, only one item was found to have an average level of competency, namely, item #5 ($\mu = 2.94, \sigma = 0.451$), 'organizational memory'.

Table 4.21: Overall Level of Skills Competency

Sl	Competency	M (μ)	S. D (σ)	NAC (%)	NC (%)	A (%)	C (%)	VC (%)	Level
1.	Technical skills	3.98	0.409	0	0	12 (5.7)	158 (74.5)	40 (18.9)	Competent
2.	Human skills	4.01	0.317	0	3 (1.4)	11 (5.2)	184 (86.8)	12 (5.7)	Competent
3.	Conceptual Skills	3.41	0.660	0	0	9 (4.2)	189 (89.2)	12 (5.7)	Competent

Source: Computed from primary data.

NAV = Not at all Competent, NC = Not Competent, N = Neutral, C = Competent, and HC = Highly Competent

Table 4.21 indicates the overall competency level of private bank employees based on the skills factors. An analysis of the results indicates that all the factors, such as technical skills ($\mu = 3.98, \sigma = 0.409$), human skills ($\mu = 4.01, \sigma = 0.317$), and conceptual skills ($\mu = 3.41, \sigma = 0.660$) of employees are found competent in performing their duties and responsibilities.

Table 4.22: Overall level of Self Concept Skills

Sl	Competency	M (μ)	S. D (σ)	NAC (%)	NC (%)	A (%)	C (%)	VC (%)	Level
1.	The imagination of our appearance to the other person	3.02	0.503	0	3 (1.4)	134 (63.2)	56 (26.4)	17 (8.0)	Average
2.	The imagination of his judgment of that appearance.	1.23	0.543	0	24 (11.3)	157 (74.1)	29 (13.7)	0	Average
3.	Some sort of self-feeling such as pride or mortification	3.95	0.932	0	0	173 (81.6)	25 (11.8)	12 (5.7)	Average

Sources: Computed from primary data.

NAV = Not at all Competent, NC = Not Competent, N = Neutral, C = Competent, and HC = Highly Competent

From table 4.22, the employee's competency level was highlighted based on three variables. It was found that of the total, all the competency parameters on self-concept parameters #1 ($\mu = 3.02$, $\sigma = 0.503$), 'the imagination of our appearance to the other person' item #2 ($\mu = 1.23$, $\sigma = 0.543$),'the imagination of his judgment of that appearance', #3 ($\mu = 3.95$, $\sigma = 0.932$),'some sort of self-feeling such as pride or mortification', are found to have average competency level.

Table 4.23: Overall Performance on Traits- Agreeable Skills (A)

Sl	Reasons	M (μ)	S. D (σ)	NAC (%)	NC (%)	A (%)	C (%)	VC (%)	Level
1.	Forgiving	4.61	0.992	1 (0.5)	13 (6.1)	51 (24.1)	75 (35.4)	70 (33)	Competent
2.	Straight forward	3.57	1.165	6 (2.8)	24 (11.3)	52 (24.5)	92 (43.4)	36 (17)	Competent
3.	Compliant in nature	3.72	1.174	7 (3.3)	39 (18.4)	47 (22.2)	61 (28.8)	56 (26.4)	Competent
4.	Modest	4.30	0.468	8 (3.8)	30 (14.2)	43 (20.3)	60 (28.3)	69 (32.5)	Very Competent

Source: Computed from primary data

NAV = Not at all Competent, NC = Not Competent, N = Neutral, C = Competent, and HC = Highly Competent

Table 4.23 reveals an employee's overall performance based on the traits (agreeable skills) in the study area. The study shows that the employee's competency on three (3) variables is found to be competent, namely item #1 (μ = 4.61, σ = 0.992) 'forgiving', item #2 (μ = 3.57, σ = 1.165)'straight forward', and #3 (μ = 3.72, σ = 1.174) 'compliant in nature'. Item #4 (μ = 4.30, σ = 0.468)'modest' is found to be very highly competent.

Table 4.24: Overall Performance on Traits-Conscientiousness Skills

Sl	Reasons	M (μ)	S. D (σ)	NAC (%)	NC (%)	A (%)	C (%)	VC (%)	Level
1.	Competent	4.30	0.759	8 (3.8)	30 (14.2)	43 (20.3)	60 (28.3	69 (32.5)	Very Com-petent
2.	Organized	4.37	0.759	0	0	1 (0.5)	146 (68.9)	63 (29.7)	Com-petent
3.	Dutiful	4.37	0.646	0	7 (3.3)	17 (8.0)	91 (42.9)	95 (44.8)	Very com-petent
4.	Achievement Striving	4.11	0.889	0	1 (0.5)	16 (7.5)	96 (45.3)	97 (45.8)	Very com-petent
5.	Self-disciplined	4.28	0.707	4 (1.9)	11 (5.2)	15 (7.1)	107 (50.5)	73 (34.4)	Com-petent

Source: Computed from primary data.

NAV = Not at all Competent, NC = Not Competent, N = Neutral, C = Competent, and HC = Highly Competent

Table 4.24 determines the private bank employee's competency level across all levels of management. An analysis result showcases the agreement variables of 5 items, and the construct-level impact was from a point scale of not at all competent to very competent. The study indicates the agreement level of 3 items was found to be very competent based on the KSA score parameter in taking up the role responsibility of employees, namely, item #1 (μ = 4.30, σ = 0.759) 'competent (C)', item #3 (μ = 4.37, σ = 0.646) 'duty', and item

#4 (μ = 4.11, σ = 0.889) 'achievement striving'. There are two parameters where the competency level of the employee's is found competent, namely item #2 (μ = 4.37, σ = 0.759) 'organized' and item #5 (μ = 4.28, σ= 0.707) 'self-discipline'.

Table 4.25: Traits- Emotional Stability Skills

Sl	Com-petent	M (μ)	S. D (σ)	NVC (%)	NAC (%)	A (%)	C (%)	VC (%)	Level
1.	Irritable (ES)	2.98	0.103	12 (5.7)	63 (29.7)	66 (31.1)	55 (25.9)	14 (6.6)	Average
2.	Depressed	2.71	0.722	10 (4.7)	63 (29.7)	114 (53.8)	23 (10.8)	0	Average
3.	Self-Conscious	2.81	1.246	6 (2.8)	31 (14.6)	9 (4.2)	127 (59.9)	37 (17.5)	Competent
4.	Impulsive	3.29	1.258	90 (42.5)	44 (20.8)	31 (14.6)	39 (18.4)	6 (2.8)	Not Very Competent

Source: Computed from primary data

NAV = Not at all Competent, NC = Not Competent, N = Neutral, C = Competent, and HC = Highly Competent

Table 4.25 determined the performance level of the employee's; an analysis result indicates the agreement variables of 4 items; and the construct-level impact was from a point scale of not at all very competent to very competent. The study shows the agreement level of 2 items was found to be average competency based on the KSA score parameter in taking up the role responsibility of employees, namely, item #1 (μ = 2.98, σ = 0.103) 'irritable' and item #2 (μ = 2.71, σ= 0.722) 'depressed'. Each item is competent, such as self-consciousness item #3, (μ = 2.81, σ = 1.246), and not very competent for the impulsive parameter, item #4, (μ= 3.29, σ = 1.258).

Table 4.26: Overall Competency Level on Traits- Extroversion Skills (E)

Sl	Reasons	M (μ)	S. D (σ)	NAC (%)	NC (%)	A (%)	C (%)	VC (%)	Level
1.	Gregarious (sociable) in nature (E)	2.73	1.118	24 (11.3)	37 (17.5)	39 (18.4)	75 (35.4)	35 (16.5)	Com-petent
2.	Assertive (forceful) in nature (E)	3.60	1.081	24 (11.30)	78 (36.8)	53 (25)	40 (18.9)	15 (7.1)	Not Com-petent
3.	Energetic in nature (E)	3.36	1.197	6 (2.8)	30 (14.2)	55 (25.9)	70 (33)	49 (23.1)	Com-petent

4.	Enthusiastic (E)	3.12	0.619	14(6.6)	40 (18.9)	57 (26.9)	55 (25.9)	44 (20.8)	Average
5.	Outgoing (E)	3.19	1.146	17(8)	42 (19.8)	48 (22.6)	68 (32.1)	35 (16.5)	Com-petent

Source: Computed from primary data

NAV = Not at all Competent, NC = Not Competent, N = Neutral, C = Competent, and VC = Very Competent

Table 4.26 endeavors to highlight the employee's overall competency level based on traits-extroversion skills; a study indicates the level of competency variables of 5 items, and the level impact was from a point scale of not very competent to very competent. An analysis shows the agreement level of 3 items was found to be competency level, namely, item #1 ($\mu = 2.73$, $\sigma = 1.118$) 'gregarious(sociable) in nature (E)', item #3 ($\mu = 3.36$, $\sigma = 1.197$) 'energetic in nature (E)', and item #5 ($\mu = 3.19$, $\sigma = 1.46$) 'outgoing'. Each one for not competent item #2 ($\mu = 3.60$, $\sigma = 1.081$) is 'assertive in nature, and average competency item #4 ($\mu = 3.12$, $\sigma = 0.619$) is 'enthusiastic'.

Table 4.27: Employees Overall Competency Level on Openness to Experience (O)

Sl	Reasons	M (μ)	S. D (σ)	NAC (%)	NC (%)	A (%)	C (%)	VC (%)	Level
1.	Curious (O)	3.12	.619	0	18 (8.6)	160 (76.2)	21 (10)	11 (5.2)	Average
2.	Person of wide interest (O)	3.19	1.146	20 (9.5)	35 (16.7)	66 (31.4)	63 (30)	26 (12.4)	Average

Table 4.27 displays that 'curious' ($\mu = 3.12$, $\sigma = .619$) and 'person of wide interest' ($\mu = 3.19$, $\sigma = 1.146$) shows the competency response at average level.

Table 4.28: Employees Overall Competency Level on Motives(Extrinsic and Intrinsic)

Sl	Variables	M (μ)	S. D (σ)	NAC (%)	NC (%)	A (%)	C (%)	VC (%)	Level
1.	Company policy and administration	4.58	0.646	20 (9.4)	35 (16.5)	66 (31.1)	63 (29.7)	26 (12.3)	Average
2.	Interpersonal relationship with supervisors	4.01	0.512	2 (0.9)	15 (7.1)	124 (58.5)	64 (30.2)	5 (2.4)	Average
3.	Interpersonal relationship with peers	4.12	0.366	0	0	18 (8.5)	53 (25)	139 (65.6)	Very Com-petent
4.	Interpersonal relationship with sub-ordinates	4.89	0.455	0	0	21 (9.9)	157 (74.1)	31 (14.6)	Com-petent
5.	Salary	2.38	0.689	0	0	3 (1.4)	179 (84.4)	28 (13.2)	Com-petent
6.	Job security	3.53	0.726	0	0	35 (16.5)	164 (77.4)	11 (5.2)	Com-petent
7.	Personal life	3.46	0.685	0	156 (73.6)	29 (13.7)	25 (11.8)	0	Not com-petent
8.	Working conditions	4.03	0.458	0	26 (12.3)	49 (23.1)	132 (62.3)	3 (1.4)	Com-petent
9.	Status	4.08	0.619	0	18 (8.5)	82 (38.7)	105 (49.5)	2 (.9)	Com-petent
10.	Achievement	3.07	0.649	0	37 (17.5)	121 (57.1)	52 (24.5)	0	Average
11.	Recognition	3.86	0.756	10 (4.7)	42 (19.8)	123 (58)	33 (15.6)	2 (0.9)	Average
12.	Advancement	3.30	0.836	0	43 (20.3)	69 (32.5)	90 (42.5)	8 (3.8)	Com-petent
13.	Work itself	3.57	0.817	7 (3.3)	21 (9.9)	29 (13.7)	151 (71.2)	2 (0.9)	Com-petent
14.	Possibility of growth	3.72	0.892	0.529	8 (3.8)	43 (20.3)	159 (75)	0	Com-petent
15.	Responsibility	4.69	0.661	0	5 (2.4)	8 (3.8)	35 (16.5)	162 (76.4)	Very com-petent

Source: Computed from primary data

NAV = Not at all Competent, NC = Not Competent, N = Neutral, C = Competent, and HC = Highly Competent

Table 4.28 analysis result indicates the agreement variables with the 15 items, and the construct-level impact was from a point scale of not very competent to very competent. The respondents agreement level of 8 items was found to be competent in the motivation parameters, namely, item #4(μ=4.89, σ =0.455) 'interpersonal relationship with subordinates' item #5 (μ = 2.38, σ = 0.689). 'salary', item # 6 (μ = 3.53, σ = 0.726) 'job security', item # 8 (μ = 4.03, σ = 0.458) 'working condition', and item # 9 (μ = 4.08, σ= 0.619)'status', item #12 (μ = 3.30, σ = 0.836) 'advancement', item #13 (μ = 3.57, σ = 0.836) 'work life', and item #14 (μ = 3.72, σ = 0.892) 'possibility of growth.

The study also highlights the existence of four items of the overall performance of the employees level that are found to be average, such as item #1 (μ = 4.58, σ = 0.646), 'company policy and administration', and item #2 (μ = 4.01, σ = 0.512), 'interpersonal relationship with supervisors, item #10 (μ = 3.07, σ = 0.649) 'achievement' and item#11 (μ = 3.86, σ =0.756)'recognition'.

The employees are found to be very competent in items # 3(μ = 3.86, σ =0.756)' interpersonal relationship with peers' and item#15 (μ = 4.69, σ =0.661) 'responsibility' and not competent in items #7 (μ = 3.46, σ =0.685) 'personal life'.

4.5 ANOVA Analysis

An attempt is made to measure the variance of the population in different scores, initially noting the significant differences between the variables based on selected banks. The results of the one-way analysis of variance are herewith as follows:

Table 4.29: Significance of Difference in Mean Score of employees competency level across selected banks on the parameter of Knowledge

Variables		Sum of square	Df	Mean Square	F	Sig.
Customer Knowledge	Between Groups	0.905	2	0.452	3.805	0.027
	Within Groups	7.967	67	0.119		
	Total	8.871	69			
Knowledge in products and services	Between Groups	1.905	2	0.952	1.161	0.319
	Within Groups	54.967	67	0.820		
	Total	56.871	69			
Knowledge in process	Between Groups	0.163	2	0.085	0.487	0.616
	Within Groups	11.617	67	0.173		
	Total	11.786	69			
Organizational memory	Between Groups	0.076	2	0.653	0.0389	0.679
	Within Groups	6.567	67	0.575		
	Total	6.643	69			
Knowledge in relationship	Between Groups	2.179	2	4.436	0.145	0.865
	Within Groups	21.257	67	0.905		
	Total	23.436	69			

In Table 4.29 'knowledge in products and services' (F=1.161, p=0.319), 'knowledge in process' (F=0.487, p=0.616), Organizational memory (F=0.0389, p=0.679), and 'knowledge in relationship (F=0.145, p=0.865) there is no significant difference at 5% level which means all the bank employees taken into consideration exhibit same level of competency under the above mentioned variables under knowledge dimension.

Regarding variable 'customer knowledge' (F=3.805, p=0.027) there is a significant difference at 5% level. An investigation result indicates that the overall competency level of HDFC Bank employees (μ = 4.10) stood highest on customer knowledge competency among the bank employees across selected banks, followed by ICICI Bank employees (μ = 3.97), and the least competency level was found among Axis Bank employees (μ= 3.80) in the north-east region.

Table 4.30 gives the impression that 'conceptual skills' (F=.0174, p=.840), there is no significant difference at 5% level which means they are exhibiting more or less same level of competency in this variable.

Table 4.30: Significance of Difference in Mean Score of employees competency level across selected banks on the parameter of Skills

Variables		Sum of square	Df	Mean Square	F	Sig.
Technical skills	Between Groups	0.922	2	1.784	10.301	.000
	Within Groups	21.196	67	0.656		
	Total	21.119	69			
Human skills	Between Groups	9.407	2	3.881	3.011	.056
	Within Groups	30.032	67	0.947		
	Total	39.439	69			
Conceptual skills	Between Groups	4.209	2	6.842	.0174	.840
	Within Groups	26.788	67	0.965		
	Total	30.997	69			

'Technical skills' with (F=10.301, p=.000) implies that the employees exhibit significant difference at 5% level which gives us a direction to compare their mean scores. A further investigation in mean score leads us that HDFC Bank is the highest (μ=4.35) followed by ICICI Bank (μ=4.17) and Axis Bank (μ=3.75).

The parameter based on 'Human Skill', the study observed that there is a significant difference among the bank's employees competency (F=3.011, p=0.056) at the significant level of 5%. HDFC bank employees with the calculated mean score of (μ = 4.15) were found to have the highest mean score; the employees are outshined in their competency compared to other bank employees; ICICI employees with a mean score of (μ = 4.00) and Axis bank employees with a mean score of (μ =3.80) stood at the least competency level.

Table 4.31: Significance of Difference in Mean Score ofemployees competency level across selected banks on the parameter of Self Concept

Variables		Sum of square	Df	Mean Square	F	Sig.
The imagination of our appearance to the other person	Between Groups	5.926	2	1.185	0.665	0.518
	Within Groups	20.924	67	0.761		
	Total	25.851	69			
The imagination of his judgment of that appearance	Between Groups	8.443	2	2.289	2.756	.071
	Within Groups	20.529	67	1.117		
	Total	28.973	69			

Some sort of self-feeling such as pride or mortification	Between Groups	4.896	2	9.379	.458	.634
	Within Groups	33.043	67	1.047		
	Total	38.939	69			

Source: Computed from primary data

In Table 4.31, Concerning to the parameter 'the imagination of our appearance to the other person' (F=0.665, p=0.518), 'The imagination of his judgment of that appearance' (F=2.756, p=.071) and 'some sort of self–feeling such as pride or mortification' (F=.458, p=.634) shows no significant level at 5% level, which means all the banks are equally exhibiting their competency in this given parameters.

Table 4.32: Significance of Difference in Mean Score of employees competency level across selected banks on the parameter of Traits–Agreeable (A) Dimension

Variables		Sum of square	Df	Mean Square	F	Sig.
Forgiving (A)	Between Groups	14.893	2	7.446	30.702	.000
	Within Groups	16.250	67	.243		
	Total	31.143	69			
Straight forward (A)	Between Groups	5.055	2	2.527	3.123	.050
	Within Groups	54.217	67	.809		
	Total	59.271	69			
Compliant in nature(A)	Between Groups	6.255	2	3.127	2.793	.068
	Within Groups	75.017	67	1.120		
	Total	81.271	69			
Modest (A)	Between Groups	1.255	2	.627	.431	.652
	Within Groups	97.617	67	1.457		
	Total	98.871	69			

Source: Computed from primary data.

Table 4.32 depicts the level of significance for selected variables under the dimension of Agreeableness. 'Forgiving' shows a high level of significance with (F=30.702, p=.000) at 5% level. Digging further into their mean scores indicate that Axis Bank (μ=4.90) is more forgiving, HDFC Bank (μ=4.75) leads the second and ICICI Bank (μ=3.9) stands in the third place.

'Straight forward' also depicts a high level of significance with (F=3.123, p=.050) at 5 % level of significance. A comparison in the mean scores shows that HDFC Bank (μ=3.70), Axis Bank (μ=3.65), ICICI Bank (μ=3.13) holds the first, second and third place respectively.

The variables 'compliant in nature' (F=2.793, p=.068) and modest (F=.431, p=.652) shows no significant difference at 5% which means all the bankers taken under consideration under the above selected variables show almost equal competency or no competency across north eastern region.

Table 4.33: Significance of Difference in Mean Score of employees competency level across selected banks on the parameter of Traits–Conscientiousness (C) Dimension

Variables		Sum of square	Df	Mean Square	F	Sig.
Competent (C)	Between Groups	1.771	2	.886	3.372	.040
	Within Groups	17.600	67	.263		
	Total	19.371	69			
Organized (C)	Between Groups	3.505	2	1.752	5.273	.007
	Within Groups	22.267	67	.332		
	Total	25.771	69			
Dutiful(C)	Between Groups	1.543	2	.771	1.620	.206
	Within Groups	31.900	67	.476		
	Total	33.443	69			
Achievement striving (C)	Between Groups	17.476	2	8.738	16.415	.000
	Within Groups	35.667	67	.532		
	Total	53.143	69			
Self-disciplined (C)	Between Groups	.443	2	.221	.450	.640
	Within Groups	33.000	67	.493		
	Total	33.443	69			

Source: Computed from primary data.

Table 4.33 shows the ANOVA table for Conscientiousness Dimension. 'Dutiful' with (F=1.620, p=.206) and 'self-disciplined' (F=.450, p= .640) shows there is no significant difference at 5% level which means all the selected bank employees are performing their duties equally and are equally self-disciplined.

The variable 'competent' with (F=3.372, p=.040) leads us to a direction that there exists a significant difference at 5% level. A comparison in the means scores between the three banks reflects that HDFC Bank is highly competent with (μ=4.70), followed by ICICI Bank (μ=4.60) and Axis Bank is least competent with (μ=4.30)

'Organized' is highly significant with (F=5.273, p= .007) at 5% level. Axis Bank employees are more organized with (μ=4.40), followed by HDFC Bank (μ= 4.00) and ICICI Bank is found to be least organized (μ=3.87)

'Achievement striving' is also found to be highly significant with (F=16.415, p=.000). A higher mean score (μ=5.00) for HDFC Bank indicates they are more achievement oriented followed by ICICI Bank (μ=4.53) and Axis Bank takes the third place with (μ= 3.7)

Table 4.34: Significance of Difference in Mean Score of employees' competency level across selected banks on the parameter of Traits – Emotional Stability(ES) Dimension

Variables		Sum of square	Df	Mean Square	F	Sig.
Irritable (ES)	Between Groups	.283	2	.142	.136	.873
	Within Groups	70.017	67	1.045		
	Total	70.300	69			
Depressed (ES)	Between Groups	.636	2	.318	.554	.577
	Within Groups	38.450	67	.574		
	Total	39.086	69			
Self-conscious (ES)	Between Groups	15.655	2	7.827	14.892	.000
	Within Groups	35.217	67	.526		
	Total	50.871	69			
Impulsive (ES)	Between Groups	61.986	2	30.993	45.638	.000
	Within Groups	45.500	67	.679		
	Total	107.486	69			

Source: Computed from primary data.

In Table 4.34, variables such as 'irritable' (F= .136, p=.873) and depressed (F= .554, p=.577) are found to be of no significant differences at 5% level.

'Self-conscious' has (F=14.892, p=.000) which means we are rejecting the null hypothesis. Comparing the mean scores it is found that Axis Bank employees are found be more self-conscious with (μ=4.65) followed by HDFC (μ=4.20) and ICICI (μ=3.53).

'Impulsive' has (F=45.638, p=.000) which is found to be highly significant at 5% level. HDFC employees are found to be more impulsive with (μ=2.95) followed by Axis (μ=2.85) and ICICI Bank (μ=1.00)

Table 4.35: Significance of Difference in Mean Score of employees competency level across selected banks on the parameter of Traits – Extroversion(E) and Openness to Experience Dimension

Variables		Sum of square	Df	Mean Square	F	Sig.
Gregarious (sociable) in nature (E)	Between Groups	33.426	2	16.713	22.210	.000
	Within Groups	50.417	67	.752		
	Total	83.843	69			
Assertive (forceful) in nature (E)	Between Groups	5.255	2	2.627	3.606	.033
	Within Groups	48.817	67	.729		
	Total	54.071	69			
Energetic in nature (E)	Between Groups	1.369	2	.685	.572	.567
	Within Groups	80.117	67	1.196		
	Total	81.486	69			
Enthusiastic (E)	Between Groups	.721	2	.361	.245	.783
	Within Groups	98.650	67	1.472		
	Total	99.371	69			
Outgoing (E)	Between Groups	5.026	2	2.513	3.340	.041
	Within Groups	50.417	67	.752		
	Total	55.443	69			
Curious (O)	Between Groups	.019	2	.010	.058	.944
	Within Groups	10.967	67	.164		
	Total	10.986	69			
Person of wide interests (O)	Between Groups	2.405	2	1.202	1.048	.356
	Within Groups	76.867	67	1.147		
	Total	79.271	69			

Source: Computed from primary data

Table 4.36 shows the ANOVA table for Extroversion Dimension. The variables 'Energetic in nature' (F=.572, p=.567), 'enthusiastic' (F=.245, p=.783), 'curious' (F=.058, p=.944) and 'person of wide interest' (F=1.048, p=.356) shows no significant mean score difference was found in competency level at 5% level. The derived outcomes from the parameters indicate that the employees from HDFC, ICICI and Axis Banks have no significant difference in their competency level. The employees exhibit equal competency across the selected banks in north eastern region. 'Gregarious' variable has (F=22.210, p=.000) which indicates there is a significant difference at 5% level. A comparison in the mean scores between the banks shows that HDFC Bank (μ=4.80) is the highest, Axis Bank (μ=4.65) is the second and ICICI Bank stands third with (μ=3.33)

'Assertive in nature' (F= 3.606, p=.033) has a significant difference at 5% level. A comparison in the mean scores indicates that HDFC leads with a mean score of (μ=4.80) followed by Axis Bank (μ= 4.65) and ICICI Bank (μ=3.33)

'Outgoing' (F=3.340, p=.041) has a significant difference at 5% level. A comparison in the

mean scores indicates that ICICI Bank has the highest mean (μ=3.87) followed by HDFC Bank (μ=3.80) and Axis Bank (μ=3.25)

Table 4.37: Significance of Difference in Mean Score of employees competency level across selected banks on the parameter of Traits – Motives Dimension (Extrinsic factors)

Variables		Sum of square	Df	Mean Square	F	Sig.
Company policy and administration	Between Groups	.005	2	.002	.004	.996
	Within Groups	38.567	67	.576		
	Total	38.571	69			
Technical supervision	Between Groups	1.683	2	.842	1.772	.178
	Within Groups	31.817	67	.475		
	Total	33.500	69			
Interpersonal relationship with supervisors	Between Groups	1.150	2	.575	1.822	.170
	Within Groups	21.150	67	.316		
	Total	22.300	69			

Interpersonal relationship with peers	Between Groups	.036	2	.018	.220	.803
	Within Groups	5.450	67	.081		
	Total	5.486	69			
Interpersonal relationship with subordinates	Between Groups	.169	2	.085	.382	.684
	Within Groups	14.817	67	.221		
	Total	14.986	69			
Salary	Between Groups	.455	2	.227	.464	.631
	Within Groups	32.817	67	.490		
	Total	33.271	69			
Job security	Between Groups	.019	2	.010	.660	.520
	Within Groups	.967	67	.014		
	Total	.986	69			
Personal life	Between Groups	.405	2	.202	.866	.425
	Within Groups	15.667	67	.234		
	Total	16.071	69			
Working conditions	Between Groups	.769	2	.385	1.244	.295
	Within Groups	20.717	67	.309		
	Total	21.486	69			
Status	Between Groups	.405	2	.202	1.602	.209
	Within Groups	8.467	67	.126		
	Total	8.871	69			

Source: Computed from primary data

Table 4.38 shows the ANOVA table for Motives Dimension. The competency variables under motives such as 'company policy and administration' (F=.004, p=.996), 'technical supervision' (F=1.772, p=.178), 'interpersonal relationship with supervisors' (F=1.822, p=.170), 'interpersonal relationship with peers' (F=.220, p=.803), 'Interpersonal relationship with subordinates' (F=.382, p=.803), 'Salary' (F=.464, p=.631), 'job security' (F=.660, p=.520), 'personal life' (F=.866, p=.425), 'working conditions' (F=1.244, p=.295) and 'status' (F=1.602, p=.209) shows no significant difference at 5% level indicating all the three banks taken under consideration are equally competent in discharging the duties of the above mentioned variables.

Table 4.39: Significance of Difference in Mean Score of employees competency level across selected banks on the parameter of Traits – Motives Dimension (Intrinsic factors)

Variables		Sum of square	Df	Mean Square	F	Sig.
Achievement	Between Groups	2.443	2	1.221	2.305	.108
	Within Groups	35.500	67	.530		
	Total	37.943	69			
Recognition	Between Groups	.686	2	.343	1.552	.219
	Within Groups	14.800	67	.221		
	Total	15.486	69			
Advancement	Between Groups	3.876	2	1.938	2.137	.126
	Within Groups	60.767	67	.907		
	Total	64.643	69			
Work itself	Between Groups	3.833	2	1.917	1.956	.149
	Within Groups	65.667	67	.980		
	Total	69.500	69			
Possibility of growth	Between Groups	.105	2	.052	.238	.789
	Within Groups	14.767	67	.220		
	Total	14.871	69			
Responsibility	Between Groups	3.733	2	1.867	3.975	.023
	Within Groups	31.467	67	.470		
	Total	35.200	69			

Table 4.39 shows the competency level of the employees under intrinsic factors. 'Achievement'(F=2.305, p=.108), 'recognition' (F=1.552, p=.219), 'advancement' (F=2.137, p=.126), 'work itself' (F=1.956, p=.149), 'possibility of growth' (F=.238, p=.789) shows no significant level at 5% level.

'Responsibility' with (F=3.975, p=.023) shows there is a significant difference at 5% level. Comparing their mean scores we derive at a conclusion that Axis and HDFC bank employees are equally responsible in taking up their responsibilities (μ=5.0) followed by ICICI Bank (μ=4.53).

References

Ross, A. and Willson, V.L. (2017). Descriptive Statistics. In Basic and Advanced Statistical Tests. Sage Publishers

Anderson, T.W. and Finn, J.D. (1996). The New Statistical Analysis of Data. Springer Verlag

Fisher, R.A. (2009). Mathematical Statistics with Applications. Academic Press, Inc.

Allen, I..E. and Seaman, C..A. (2007). Likert Scales and Data Analyses. *Quality Progress.*

Brace, N., Kemp, R. andSneglar R. (2000). SPSS for Psychologists. *Macmillan press.*

Islam, M., T. (2020). Learning SPSS without Pain: A Comprehensive Guide for Data Analysis and Interpretation of Outputs (1st Edition). *ASA Publications.*

Pallant J. (2007). SPSS Survival Manual (3rd Edition). *Open University Press*

Chapter - 5

Findings and Recommendations

5.1 Introduction

The banking sector in India is essential to the country's economic growth and serves as the foundation for the expansion of the money market. Employee competency in the banking sector is the primary engine of economic development with a strong focus on customer satisfaction. In the current competitive landscape, banks are making a concerted effort to gain customer satisfaction through the provision of innovative and superior services. Banking services now place more of an emphasis on customer satisfaction and retention than on acquiring new customers, owing to the explosive growth of Internet users and the widespread use of mobile technology. **Retaining the same customers overtime requires certain Knowledge, Skills and Abilities (KSA's) of the employees that thrives towards the competency of the banks.** The study is constructed with a sample of 210 respondents from seven (7) states of North East Region, namely Meghalaya, Assam, Manipur, Arunachal Pradesh, Tripura, Mizoram, and Nagaland. The primary focus of the study is to evaluate employee competency in two categories: initial importance of the variables were evaluated by the branch manager of each bank on selected bank employees, followed by the overall competency level of employees. Systematic analysis was conducted to serve the objectives of the study, and the findings are presented stepwise herewith below:

5.2. Summary of Findings for Objective 1 based on Job Description

Findings for Objective 1 is based on Information input, Mental process, Work output, Relationship with other persons, Job context and Job related variables.

5.2.1 Findings based on Information Input

(i) Most of the respondents fall under the age group of 21-35 (45.2%) which means most of the respondents are youngsters.

(ii) The gender distribution comprising 60% male and 40 % female gives us a direction that there is no much gender bias in measuring the competencies from the bank employees across the select banks.

(iii) The study reveals that the selected states, namely Meghalaya, Assam, Arunachal Pradesh, Manipur, Tripura, Mizoram, and Nagaland, contribute a sample unit of 30 respondents from each state, a total of 210 sample size, each consisting of 14.29% from HDFC, Axis, and ICICI banks.

(iv) It was found that the mean value on the level of management was found at the 3 levels of categories, which highlights that the majority of the managerial respondents are at the lower level of management, having 3 to 4 years of service in the present organization.

(v) Based on respondents' awareness of job analysis, the study shows that the majority of the respondents fall under the construct scale of 4, meaning that respondents are aware of job analysis.

(vi) Employees' awareness of the job description exhibits a scale of 3.17 in the range of neutral to awareness level, indicating they are approximately aware of the essential roles and responsibilities associated with the job.

(vii) A construct of 4.11 indicates that the employees have knowledge of the specific job which they are performing.

(viii) A construct of 3.98 indicates that they are nearly aware of the importance of job analysis conducted by the banks.

5.2.2 Findings based on Mental Process

(i) Bringing new business is considered to be very important by the bank employees.

(ii) Most of the functions require 'human Skills' to get the work done.

(iii) The mental demand in terms of level of concentration and duration of mental effort is found to be mostly normal with 79.5 % respondents and only 20.4% claim it to be continual.

5.2.3 Findings based on Work Output

(i) 84% claimed that the level of proficiency for using the technical knowledge is advanced and 16% claimed to be intermediate. It is also to be noted that out of the three select banks, two banks uses the same software.

5.2.4 Findings based on relationship with other persons

(i) The 1st rank is given to communication with customers and staff, team work is given the 2nd rank, management of conflict situation is given the 3rd rank and sharing work responsibility is given the 4th rank.

5.2.5 Findings based on Job Context

(i) 52% of the respondents claim that they take up the level of responsibility for waste, damage, defects or other loss of value to material assets (e.g., parts, equipment, or cash) caused by inadequate job performance or inattentiveness.

5.2.6 Findings based on Job Related Variables

(i) 48.3% of the employees claim that they always receive supervision by the supervisors.

5.3. Summary of Findings for Objective 2 based on Importance of Employees Competency Level Appraised by Manager

(i) The branch managers have responded that the salary they receive is not adequate enough and this can be an alarming reason of decreasing competencies in some parameters across the banks.

(ii) Also the branch managers responded that job security, personal life and working conditions are average across all banks which means that the employees have a fear of losing jobs. Work life balance plays an important role in any job, and if the score is average in this dimension, makes us to rethink that 86.5% of the respondents are married, and whether there is an adequate balance in the personal and professional life of the employees which is having an impact on their competencies.

(iii) The Branch Managers across the select banks in north east India considers *knowledge in products and services, knowledge in relationships with customer, peer groups, subordinates and supervisors technical skills, interpersonal relationship with peers and responsibility* to be very important in competency dimension.

(iv) ANOVA results further helps us to test the significance of each parameter on the basis of importance and it is found that under customer knowledge, HDFC Bank Branch Managers found to be most important followed by ICICI and Axis Bank Branch Managers.

(v) Under agreeableness, importance is claimed most again by HDFC followed by Axis and ICICI Banks.

(vi) Under Openness to Experience, ICICI bank branch managers leads followed by Axis and HDFC Banks in rating the importance.

(vii) Importance of Technical Supervision is provided most by ICICI Bank Branch Managers followed by HDFC and Axis Banks.

(viii) Importance of Interpersonal Relationship with Supervisors is claimed mostly by ICICI Bank followed by Axis and HDFC exhibiting equal level of importance.

(ix) The importance of salary is claimed most by ICICI Bank followed by Axis and HDFC Bank exhibiting equal importance.

(x) ICICI Bank employees gives more importance to job security followed by HDFC and Axis Bank employees.

(xi) ICICI Bank Branch Managers gives highest importance to personal life followed by HDFC and Axis Banks.

(xii) The importance to responsibility is given mostly by Axis Bank Branch Managers followed by ICICI and HDFC Banks.

5.4. Summary of Findings for Objective 3 based on Overall Employee Assessment of their Competencies

5.4.1 Overall Banks Employees Competency Based on Knowledge Dimension

(i) All the variables under knowledge dimension are found to be equally competent or very competent. Only one variable 'organizational memory (organizational archives, databases and individual memories) competency is average. It is quite obvious that bank employees will not be in a position to remember all databases which is humanely quite impossible.

(ii) HDFC Bank employees are found to be more competent with regard to customer knowledge followed by ICICI and Axis Bank employees.

5.4.2 Overall Banks Employees Competency Based on Skills Dimension

(i) All the variables under skills are found to be equally competent for each bank. However, testing the significance level it is found that under technical skills HDFC is leading followed by ICICI and Axis Bank employees.

(ii) Under Human Skills HDFC is leading followed by ICICI and Axis Banks.

5.4.3 Overall Banks Employees Competency Based on Self-Concept Dimension

(i) All the variables under self-concept are found to be average in competency level. Self- concept is basically a reflection of self and what is perceived by others. It is found out that self-concept dimension is not noticeably focused upon by the employees.

5.4.4 Overall Banks Employees Competency Based on Trait Dimension

A. Agreeableness

(i) Employees are found to be equally competent in 'forgiving in nature', 'straight forward' and 'compliant' for all employees across the select banks. The employees are also found to be very competent in modest variable across the banks.

B. Conscientiousness

(i) The overall competency measures reflects that employees are very competent, organized, dutiful, achievement striving and self-disciplined.

(ii) A further analysis reflects that HDFC is more competent in 'competent' dimension followed by ICICI and Axis Banks.

(iii) Axis Bank employees are found to more organized followed by HDFC and ICICI Bank.

(iv) HDFC bank employees are found to be more achievement oriented followed by ICICI and Axis Banks.

C. Emotional Stability

(i) The employees are found to be not very competent in 'impulsive' dimension which means they do not act with no thought to outcome. Significance tests shows that HDFC leads followed by Axis and ICICI Banks. This means the employees of HDFC banks are more thoughtful followed by Axis and ICICI Banks.

D. Extroversion

(i) The overall competency measure gives us a glimpse that the employees from all the banks are found to be equally sociable, energetic and outgoing.

(ii) The employees tend to score average on enthusiastic dimension which gives us an alarm to evaluate the root causes of less enthusiasm amongst the employees.

(iii) The employees are not very assertive (forceful) in nature which is again a positive trait in employee behavior.

(iv) HDFC Banks employees are found to be more gregarious (sociable) followed by Axis and ICICI Bank.

(v) ICICI Bank employees are found to be more outgoing followed by HDFC and Axis Bank.

E. Openness to Experience

(i) The employees of all the select banks are found to be average in curiosity dimension and not employees of wide interest. This results compels us to rethink the work pressure and the monotonous job role, the over pressurizing targets and cut throat competition that acts as a barrier in their constructive thinking.

5.4.5 Overall Banks Employees Competency Based on Motives Dimension

(i) The employees are found to be very competent in sharing inter personal relationships with peers and taking up responsibility.

(ii) The employees seem to be satisfied with the relationship they share with subordinates, happy about their salary, working conditions, job security, status, advancement, work itself and possibility of growth.

(iii) The employees are not very satisfied with the achievement and recognition they receive.

(iv) The research derives at a conclusion that all the extrinsic factors of motivation are equally present in all the employees of the selected banks under consideration in North East India. Thus the bank employees of Axis, HDFC and ICICI Banks are equally competent in the given variables.

(v) Under the intrinsic factors, HDFC and Axis Bank employees are found to be taking up responsibility equally followed by ICICI Bank.

5.5 Conclusion

The research draws a conclusion that when the employees of all the three select private sector banks of North East India, namely, Axis, HDFC and ICICI Banks are taken together to assess the competencies of the employees, HDFC Bank employees are found to be leading in almost all the competency parameters followed by ICICI Bank and Axis Bank respectively. The mapping of the competencies helps us to understand the reasons why HDFC Bank is leading in the Private Banking Sector over the years. Competency mapping also helped to understand the reasons for the other two banks to further dig into themselves and analyze the competency parameters where they need to work upon. Job description gives a direction in the research to summarize the roles and responsibilities associated with the work. Job description helps us to gather basic information about the work undertaken in the banking sector and to what extent is the mental requirement of the job. Competency mapping gives us a clear picture that the employees from all the select banks scored average on job security, personal life and working conditions, which is alarming from employee satisfaction. The overall evaluation of competencies and their mapping gives us an insight that knowledge in products and services, technical skills and interpersonal relationship with peers are found to be the best competencies. Concurrently, competencies such as self –concept, extroversion, trait(enthusiastic) in nature, openness to experience, personal life, and recognition needs to be focused upon.

The null hypothesis formulated for the study is:

Ho: There is no significant difference among the actual level of competencies and desired level of competencies across the banks.

(a) It is observed that in *knowledge* dimension, out of the five variables only customer knowledge is found to be significant. Thus the null hypothesis is rejected and we accept the alternative hypothesis.

(b) Under *skills* dimension, out of human, conceptual and technical skills, only technical skill is found to be significant. Thus the null hypothesis is rejected and we accept the alternative hypothesis.

(c) Under *self-concept dimension*, there is no significant difference at 5% level for all the three variables. Thus we accept the null hypothesis and reject the alternative hypothesis.

(d) Under *Traits* dimension, Agreeableness, out of 4 variables only two are found to be significant. Thus we reject the null hypothesis and accept the alternative hypothesis

(e) Under Conscientiousness Dimension, out of 5 variables, only 3 are found to be significant. Thus we reject the null hypothesis and accept the alternative hypothesis.

(f) Under Emotional Stability, out of 4 factors only two are found to be significant. Thus we reject the null hypothesis and accept the alternative hypothesis.

(g) Under Extroversion, out of 5 factors, 3 are found to be significant. Thus we reject the null hypothesis and accept the alternative hypothesis.

(h) Under Openness to Experience, out of 2 factors, none of the factors are found to be significant, thus we accept the null hypothesis and reject the alternative hypothesis.

(i) Under 10 *Extrinsic factors of motivation*, none of the factors are found to have significant difference. Thus we accept the null hypothesis and reject the alternative hypothesis.

(j) Under 6 *Intrinsic factors of motivation*, only 1 factor is found to have significant difference. Thus we reject the null hypothesis and accept the alternative hypothesis.

(k) Assessing the Iceberg model of competencies, it is found that all the employees from Axis , HDFC and ICICI Banks are found to be competent under visible skills, i.e Knowledge and Skills, but under invisible factors, i.e self–concept, traits and motives there are few variables like irritable, depressed, enthusiastic, openness to experience, company policy and administrations, relationship with supervisors, achievement and recognition scored average on these variables, which is very alarming and further research can be conducted to analyse the reasons for the same.

(l) Also when significant test was conducted it was found that HDFC Banks leads in most of the parameters followed by ICICI and Axis Banks.

(m) Tukey's Honestly Significant Post Hoc Test could not be conducted after ANOVA as all the factors are not found to be significant which is a pre determining condition for the test.

5.6 Limitation of the Study

The research draws a limitation that only three private sector banks have been taken for the purpose of the research. However, if more private sector banks could have been considered the results would have given more degree of variation. Also the geographical location of the states and its accessibility provided a hindrance as the hard copy of the questionnaire could not be provided. But Google Forms came to the rescue in reaching the employees of select banks across corners of North East India.

5.7 Scope of Further Research

(a) Research can be undertaken in this field with consideration of a larger sample unit across various sectors of banks.

(b) A comparative study of competency can be conducted across public and private sector banks.

(c) Each dimension of competency taken under the Iceberg Model of Competencies can be studied as a separate unit.

(d) A comparative study between the visible and invisible set of competencies can also be studied separately.

5.8 Social Relevance of the Study

(a) The study focuses on the competency level of bank employees in seven states of selected private banks operating in the north east region. It is primarily emphasized by three bank employees, namely HDFC, ICICI, and Axis Bank.

(b) The study on understanding competency aims to improve banking performance and create quality services for customers. Many people have complaints about how staff members handle the increasing number of customers and the current state of limited tangible infrastructure.

(c) Customers are able to comprehend the system effectively because they are navigating a number of operational and environmental chains. Additionally, it made consumers more conscious of the need to reduce their exploitation and free themselves from the ignorance that surrounds them.

(d) The study helped bank management gain a wide range of insights that helped them tailor their customer outreach strategies. Further, it also helps them to carry out different growth, expansion, and promotions in order to successfully draw clients.

References

Abzari, M., Shahin, A., & Abasaltian, A. (2016). Studying the impact of personality constructs on employees' knowledge sharing behavior through considering the mediating role of intelligent competencies in project-oriented organizations. *Modern Applied Science*, *10*(6), 194-204.

Ahmad, Z. (2016). *Education 2030 Launch and Symposium. Malaysia Ministry of Education, (August)*. Retrieved from https://www.moe.gov.my/images/Terbitan/Rujukan-Akademik/Presentation-Education-2030-Launch-Symposium-23rd-August-2016-Hotel-Istana-Ballroom-Kuala-Lumpur/Zanariah-Hj-Ahmad/Zanariah Hj. Ahmad.pdf

Ajitabh, A., & Momaya, K. (2004). Competitiveness of firms: review of theory, frameworks and models. *Singapore management review*, *26*(1), 45-61.

Allen, I..E. and Seaman, C..A. (2007). Likert Scales and Data Analyses. *Quality Progress* and Background of the Position Analysis Questionnaire (PAQ). *Occupational Research Center.*

Anderson, T.W. and Finn, J.D.(1996). The New Statistical Analysis of Data. Springer Verlag.

Aralihond, T. and Battur, A. (2020). A Study on Competency Mapping of B-School Students For Employability. *International E Conference on Adapting to the New Business Normal – The way ahead December 3-4, 2020 Mysuru, India*

Asumeng, M.A. (2014). Managerial Competency Models: A critical review and proposed holistic –domain model, *Journal of Management Research, Las Vegas, Nev: Macrothink Institute*, *6*(4), 1-20.

Atkinson, S.P. (2015). Graduate Competencies, Employability and Educational Taxonomies: Critique of Intended Learning Outcomes. *Practice and Evidence of Scholarship of Teaching and Learning in Higher Education, 10*(2),154-177

Axis Bank Press Release, August 23, 2022. https://www.axisbank.com/about-us/press-releases/axis-bank-dedicates-four-new-branches-in-the-north-east-in-the-presence-of-hon-finance-minister-of-india-nirmala-sitharaman

Axis Bank (2023). Annual Reports, Axis Bank. https://www.axisbank.com/docs/default-source/annual-reports/for-axis-bank/annual-report-for-the-year-2022-2023.pdf

Ayonmike, C. S. O., Chijioke, P., & Okeke, B. C. (2014). Competency based education and training in technical vocational education: Implication for sustainable national security and development. *Journal of Educational Policy and Entrepreneurial Research*, *1*(2), 290-300.

Aziz, Z.A. (2005).*Developing a robust competency framework for the Malaysian banking industry Opening speech by Dr Zeti Akhtar Aziz,* Governor of the Central Bank of Malaysia, at the Industry Competency Framework Study Focus Group Discussion, Kualaumpur, 6 December 2005. BIS Review 83/2005

Barrick, M. R., Mount, M. K., & Judge, T. A. (2001). Personality and performance at the beginning of the new millennium: What do we know and where do we go next? *International Journal of Selection and assessment*, *9*(1-2), 9-30.

Bartram, D. (2005). The Great Eight competencies: a criterion-centric approach to validation. *Journal of applied psychology*, *90*(6), 1185.

Bath, D., Smith, C., Stein, C. and Swann, R. (2004). Beyond mapping and embedding graduate attributes: bringing together quality assurance and action learning to create a validated and living curriculum, *Higher Education Research & Development, 23*(3), 313-328.

Berio, G., & Harzallah, M. (2007). Towards an integrating architecture for competence management. *Computers in Industry*, *58*(2), 199-209.

Bhandari, G.S. (2018). A Study on the Banking Sector Scenario of the North-East Region of India. Anveshak, International Journal of Management, *7*(1), 9-22.

Bharadwaj. et.al (2019). Competency Mapping Based on Identifying the Impact over the Productivity of SMEs. International Journal of Innovative Technology and Exploring Engineering (IJITEE), *9*(2), 2236.

Bharthvajan, R. (2013). Competency mapping. *International Journal of Innovative Research in Science, Engineering and Technology, 2*(11), 6288-6294.

Bodnarchuk, M. (2012). The role of job descriptions and competencies in an international organization: Case: Foster Wheeler EnergiaOy.

Boro, K. (2015), "Prospects and challenges of technological innovation in banking industry of North East India", *Journal of Internet Banking and Commerce*, October

Boucher, X., Bonjour, E. and Matta, N. (2007).Competence Management in Industrial Processes. *Computers in Industry*. *58*(2), 95-97

Boyatzis, R. E. (1982). *The Competent Manager: A Model for Effective Performance*. New Delhi: New Age International Private Limited.

Boyatzis, R.E. (2009), "Competencies as a behavioral approach to emotional intelligence",Journal of Management Development, Vol. 28, No. 9.

Boyatzis, R. E(2007) Competencies in the 21st century, *Journal of Management Development,27* (1), 5-12.

Brace, N., Kemp, R. and Sneglar R. (2000). SPSS for Psychologists. *Macmillan press*.

Branham, L. (2005). *The 7 Hidden Reasons Employees Leave*. Pensylvannia: Sound view Executive Book Summaries.

Bratton, J. (2007). Strategic human resource management. *Human Resource Management içinde, Der: John Bratton,-Gold, Jeffrey, London: Palgrave Macmillan, London*, 37-71.

Bücker, J., & Poutsma, E. (2010). Global management competencies: A theoretical foundation. *Journal of Managerial Psychology*, *25*(8), 829-844.

Burgoyne, J.G. and Stuart, R. (1976). The nature, use and acquisition of managerial skills and other attributes. *Personal Review, 5*(4), 19-20.

Burmann, C., & König, V. (2011). Does internal brand management really drive brand commitment in shared-service call centers? *Journal of brand management*, *18*(6), 374-393.

Chakma, J. K. (2014), "Financial inclusion in India: A brief focus on Northeast India", *International Journal of Application or Innovation in Engineering & Management*, *3*(11)

Chakrabarty, K.C. (2009), "Banking: key driver for inclusive growth", *RBI Monthly Bulletin, 9.*

Chakravorty, D. and Ahmed, J.U. (2020). Knowledge Management as a parameter of Competency Mapping: A Study in HDFC Bank Ltd. Operating at Silchar, Assam. In Akoijam, S.L.S, Sharma, L. S, Ahmed, J.U. and Singh, W.C. (Eds), *Dynamics of Sustainable Business Management: Perspectives and Strategies* (pp. 229-242). Mittal Publications.

Chakravorty, D. and Ahmed, J.U. (2024). The Influence of Big Five Personality Traits on the Competencies of the Bank Employees: A Study on Private Bank Employees of North East India. *ISAR Journal of Economics and Business Management, 2*(2), 1-7. https://isarpublisher.com/journal/isarjebm

Chakravorty, D. and Ahmed, J.U. (2022). Competitive Banking Environment: A Study on Private Sector Banks in Tura Region of Meghalaya. In Kakati, R.P. and Mahanta, M. (Eds), *Business Practices in the Age of Innovation, Disruption and Sustainability, 2*, (pp. 115-119*)*. Excel Publishers.

Chakravorty, D., Ahmed, J. U. and Chakravarty, D. (2023). Assessing Herzberg's Theory in Private Banking: A Competency Study. *International Journal of Science and Research (IJSR), 12*(12), 58-63. https://dx.doi.org/10.21275/SR231124183219

Chandekar, M and Jain, S.K. (2015). Competency Mapping: A Strategic tool in employee Recruitment. *Abhinav International Monthly Refereed Journal of Research in Management & Technology, 4*(1), 27-33.

Choudhary, S and Singh, S. (2010). A Study of Competency Mapping of Employees in Banking Sector With Special Reference To ICICI Bank. *International Journal of Human Resources Management, 5*(3), 11-20.

Cooley, C. H. (1902). *Human Nature and the Social Order*. Scribner.

Currie, G. & Darby, R. (1995), "Competence-based Management Development: Rhetoric & Reality", Journal of European Industrial Training, Vol. 19, No. 5.

Damayanti, D. (2021). Human resources competency in the era of industrial revolution 4.0. *Economics and Business Solutions Journal*, *5*(1), 13-27.

Demirguc-Kunt, A. and Klapper, L. (2013), "Measuring financial inclusion: explaining variation in use of financial services across and within countries", *Brookings Papers on Economic Activity, 1*.

Dong, Y. (2023). Descriptive Statistics and its Application. *Highlights in Science, Engineering and Technology, 47,* 16-23.

Dwivedi, G. (2017). A Study Of Increasing Employee Attrition Rate Of Axis Bank: Jhalawar (Rajasthan) Region. *International Journal of Science Technology and Management, 6*(1), 732-745.

Fang, R., Landis, B., Zhang, Z., Anderson, M. H., Shaw, J. D., & Kilduff, M. (2015). Integrating personality and social networks: A meta analysis of personality, network position, and work outcomes in organizations. *Organization science*, *26*(4), 1243-1260.

Fatma, A. and Mishra, M.K. (2017). Analytical Study of Competency Mapping and Employees Effectiveness of Private Banks in Urban Jhansi. *Journal of Advances and Scholarly Researches in Allied Education, 13*(1), 1124-1126.

Fisher, R.A. (2009). Mathematical Statistics with Applications. Academic Press, Inc.

Garrett, S. (2008). *Competency Mapping: What Is It and How It Can Be Done by Individuals*. Career Trainer.

Gelani, T.C. (2015). Comprehensive Study Of Attrition Strategy Of HDFC BANK in Ahmadabad Region. *RHIMRJ*, *2*(5), 1-6.

Goetz, T., Cronjaeger, H., Frenzel, A. C., Ludtke, O., & Hall, N. C. (2010). Academic self-concept and emotion relations: Domain specificity and age effects. *Contemporary Educational Psychology*, *35*, 44–58.

Goldberg, L.R. (1990). An Alternative Description of Personality: The Big Five Factor Structure, *Journal of Personality and Social Psychology*, *59*(6), 1216-29.

Gupta, B., Iyer, L.S. and Aronson, J.E. (2000). Knowledge Management: Practices and Challenges. *Industrial Management and Data Systems*, *100*(1), 17-21.

Halder, K.U. (Ed.). (2011). *Human Resource Development* (3rd ed.). Oxford Higher Education.

Hawkes, C. L., & Weathington, B. L. (2014). Competency-Based Versus Task-Based Job Descriptions: Effects on Applicant Attraction. Journal of Behavioral and Applied Management, 15(3), 190-211.

Hayes, J.L. (1979). A new look at managerial competence: the AMA model of worthy performance. *Management Review, 68*(11), 2-3.

HDFC Bank (2023). Annual Reports, HDFC Bank. https://www.hdfcbank.com/content/bbp/repositories/723fb80a-2dde-42a3-9793-7ae1be57c87f/?path=/Footer/About%20Us/Investor%20Relation/annual%20reports/pdf/Integrated%20Annual%20Report%202022-23.pdf

Hind, D., Moss, S. and McKellan, S. (2007). Innovative Assessment Strategies for developing Employability Skills in the Tourism and Entertainment Management Curriculum at Leeds Metropolitan University. Paper presented at the Euro-CHRIE Conference, Leeds, UK.

Hsieh, S.C., Lin, J.S. and Lee, H.C. (2012). Analysis on Literature Review of Competency. *International Review of Business and Economics,* 2, 25-50.

https://www.forbesindia.com/article/explainers/top-10-banks-india-by-market-cap/87913/1.

Hu, A., Li, X., & Song, H. (2023). The influence of Big Five personality traits on college students' key competencies: the mediating effect of psychological capital. *Frontiers in Psychology, 14*.

Hu, Q. (2019, February). Analysis on the Impact of Knowledge-based Employees' Competency on Performance in E-commerce Enterprises. In *2018 International Symposium on Social Science and Management Innovation (SSMI 2018)* (pp. 545-552). Atlantis Press.

Hughes, A., Galbraith, D., & White, D. (2011). Perceived competence: A common core for self-efficacy and self-concept?. *Journal of personality assessment, 93*(3), 278-289.

IBM Analytics Datasheet (2016). Banking and Financial Services. Job Skills and Competencies Framework. https://www.redbooks.ibm.com/redbooks/pdfs/sg247908.pdf

ICICI Bank (2023). Annual Reports, ICICI Bank. https://www.icicibank.com/ms/aboutus/annual-reports/2022-23/icici/index.html

Ishak, H. (2016). Industrial Revolution 4.0 in Malaysia? "Fostering Research and Malaysian Aerospace Industry. *Factory of The Future*.

Islam, M., T. (2020). Learning SPSS without Pain: A Comprehensive Guide for Data Analysis and Interpretation of Outputs (1st Edition). *ASA Publications*.

Jain, V.K. (2013).Competency Mapping in Indian Industries - A Case Study. *International Journal of Emerging Research in Management & Technology, 2*(10), 9-21.

Jerslid, A. T. (1965). Social and original origins of the self. In D. E. Hamachek(Ed.), *The self in growth, teaching and learning* (pp. 196–208). Englewood Cliffs.

Jindal, M. and Agarwal, M. (2016). A Case Study of Axis Bank: Relationship between Empowerment and Job Satisfaction. *IJRSI, 3*(5), 122-126.

Judge, T. A., Martocchio, J. J., & Thoresen, C. J. (1997). Five-factor model of personality and employee absence. *Journal of applied psychology*, *82*(5), 745.

Kanfer, R., & Ackerman, P. L. (2005). Work competence. *Handbook of competence and motivation*, 336-353.

Kassem, M. A., Khoiry, M. A. and Hamzah, N. (2020). Using Relative Importance Index Method for Developing Risk Map in Oil and Gas Construction Projects. *Jurnal Kejuruteraan*, *32*(3), 85-97.

Katz, R.L. (1955). Skills for an Effective Administrator. *Harvard Business Review.*

Kaur, J. and Kumar, V. (2013). Competency Mapping: A Gap Analysis. *International Journal of Education and Research, 1*(1), 1-9.

Kaur, P., Stoltfuz, J. and Yellapu, P. (2018). Descriptive Statistics. *International Journal of Academic Medicine. 4(1),* 60-63.

Kaushik, M. and Mathur, B. (2014). Data Analysis of Students Marks with Descriptive Statistics. *International Journal on Recent and Innovation Trends in Computing and Communication*, *2*(5), 1188-1190.

Klemp, G.O. (ed.) (1980). *The Assessment of occupational competence,* Washington, DC, Report to National Institution of Education.

Knapp, H. (2014). Introductory Statistics using SPSS. *Sage Publications, Inc.*

Kumar, S., Nayyar, S. and Anjuman, B. (2014). Competency Mapping - A Managerial Perception (A Study of Hdfc Bank Ltd. *Journal of Social Science Research*. 3. 373-384.

Lawler III, E. E. (1994). From job-based to competency-based organizations. *Journal of organizational behavior*, *15*(1), 3-15.

Lawler III, Edward, E. (1994). From job-based to competency-based organizations. *Journal of organizational behavior*, *15*(1), 3-15.

Lawler, E. E. (1984). The strategic design of reward systems. *Strategic human resource management*, *9*(1), 7-16.

Maity, S. (2019), "Financial inclusion status in North Eastern region: an evidence of commercial banks", *International Journal of Research in Applied Management, Science and Technology, 4*(3)

Makulova, A. T., Alimzhanova, G. M., Bekturganova, Z. M., Umirzakova, Z. A., Makulova, L. T., & Karymbayeva, K. M. (2015). Theory and practice of competency-based approach in education. *International Education Studies*, *8*(8), 183-192.

Manju, S., Jayanthi, D. and Kowsalya, N. (2020). Competency Mapping Among The Ites Sectors: A Study Among The Ites Employees In Coimbatore. European Journal of Molecular & Clinical Medicine, *7*(3).

Marsh, H. W. (1992). Content specificity of relations between academic achievement and academic self-concept. *Journal of educational psychology*, *84*(1), 35.

Marsh, H. W., & Shavelson, R. (1985). Self-concept: Its multifaceted, hierarchical structure. *Educational Psychologist, 20*, 107–125.

Marsh, H. W., Walker, R., & Debus, R. L. (1991). Subject-specific components academic self-concept and self-efficacy. *Contemporary Educational Psychology, 16*, 331–345.

McClelland, D. C. and Winter, D. G. (1969). *Motivating economic achievement.* Free Press.

McClelland, D.C. (1973). Testing for competence rather than for intelligence. *American Psychologist, 28*(1), 1–14.

McCormick, Ernest J.; Jeanneret, Paul R.; Mecham, Robert C. (1969). The Development.

McCrae, R. R., & Costa, P. T. (2008). Empirical and theoretical status of the five-factor model of personality traits. *The SAGE handbook of personality theory and assessment, 1*, 273-294.

Md. Ishtiak Uddin, *et. al.* (2012) Competency Mapping: A Tool for HR Excellence, European Journal of Business and Management, Vol. 4, No. 5.

Mohana kumari, D. and Magesh, R. (2017) Competency development through training and development: An empirical study,*Indian J. Sci. Res,14* (1), 69-70.

Morey, D. *et al* (2001), *Knowledge Management*. Hyderabad: University Press.

Murtaza, Z. (2015) An Empirical Study Of Competency Mapping Of The Employees In The Tourism Sector In Jammu And Kashmir-An Executive Level Perspective. *Journal of Business Management & Social Sciences Research , 4*(2), 202-208.

Nagaraju, Y and Gowda, V.S. (2012). A Study of employee competency mapping strategies at select organization of Bangalore. *International Journal of Research in commerce and management, 3*(10), 176-182.

Nair, V.V. (2014). *Behavioural Competency Management With Special Reference To Commercial Banks Headquartered In Kerala* (Doctoral Dissertation, Cochin University of Science and Technology, Kerala, India

Nebo, A. M. (2022). The application of "The Looking Glass Self" to leadership development. *Net Journal of Social Sciences,10*(1), 12-18.

Nicholas, J. (2006). Introduction to Descriptive Statistics. *Mathematics Learning Center*.

Nonaka, I and Takeuchi, H. (1995), The Knowledge-creating Company: How Japanese Companies Create the Dynamics of Innovation, Oxford University Press.

Nybø, G. (2004). Personnel development for dissolving jobs: towards a competency-based approach? *The International Journal of Human Resource Management, 15*(3), 549-564.

Ostertagova, E. and Ostertag, O. (2013). Methodology and Application of One Way ANOVA. *American Journal of Mechanical Engineering, 1(7)*, 256-261.

Pallant J. (2007). SPSS Survival Manual (3rd Edition). *Open University Press.*

Panwar, D., & Sati, M. C. (2023). Impact of Katz's Skills of Managers in School Management: A Study of Pauri District in Uttarakhand, India. *Migration Letters, 20*(S10), 508-513.

Parry, S.R. (1996). *The Quest for Competencies,* Training. *33*(7), 48-56.

Pavur Jr, E. J. (2010). Use job descriptions to support leadership. *The Psychologist-Manager Journal, 13*(2), 119-122.

Pietsch, J., Walker, R., & Chapman, E. (2003). The relationship among self-concept, self-efficacy, and performance in mathematics during secondary school. *Journal of Educational Psychology, 95*, 589–603.

Prahalad, C. K., & Hamel, G. (1994). Strategy as a field of study: Why search for a new paradigm? *Strategic management journal, 15*(S2), 5-16.

Prasad, P. (2015). Performance Appraisal: An Empirical Study to understand Job Satisfaction and Motivation of personnel through the system. International Journal of Engineering and Applied Sciences, 2(4), 118-125.

Rainsbury, E., Hodges, D., Burchell, N. and Lay, M. (2002). Ranking Workplace Competencies: Student and Graduate Perceptions, *Asia-Pacific Journal of Cooperative Education, 3*(2), 8-18.

Rajnai, Z., & Kocsis, I. (2017, September). Labor market risks of industry 4.0, digitization, robots and AI. In *2017 IEEE 15th International Symposium on Intelligent Systems and Informatics (SISY)* (pp. 000343-000346). IEEE.

Rathod, T.R. (2015). *Employees competency mapping in private sector banks a study with special reference to private sector banks in hyderabad karnataka region,* (Doctoral dissertation, Gulbarga University, Karnataka)

Ross, A. and Willson, V.L. (2017). Descriptive Statistics. In Basic and Advanced Statistical Tests. Sage Publishers.

S. El-Sabaa (2001). The Skills and Career Path of an Effective Project Manager. *International Journal of Project Management, 19*, 1-7.

Sahoo, A., & Kundrakapam, J. K. (2006), "A review of trends in banking indicators in North Eastern Region of India", *Reserve Bank of India Occasional Papers, 27*(3).

Sanghi, S. (2004). *The Handbook of Competency Mapping Understanding, Designing, and Implementing Competency Models in Organizations*. Sage Publications Inc.

Scarbrough, H. (2000). Recipe for Success. *People Management, 9*(2), 32-5.

Schippmann, J. S. (2010). Competencies, job analysis, and the next generation of modeling. *Handbook of workplace assessment, 32*, 197.

Schulz, S., & Steyn, T. (2003). Educators' motivation: Differences related to gender, age and experience. *Actaacademica, 35*(3), 138-160.

Schunk, D. H., & Pajares, F. (2002). The development of academic self-efficacy. In *Development of achievement motivation* (pp. 15-31). Academic Press.

Selznick, P. (1957). *Leadership in Administration: A Sociological Interpretation*. University of California.

Shannon, R. (2005). Herzberg's Two-Factor Theory of Motivation applied to the motivational techniques within financial institutions". Senior Honors Theses & Projects. 119.

Sharma, N. and Khanna, K. (2015). Competency Mapping. *Paripex-Indian Journal of Research, 4*(1), 161-163.

Sheskin, D.J. (Ed.). (2007). Handbook of Parametric and Nonparametric Statistical Procedures. (4th Ed.). *Chapman and Hall/CRC*

Shree, B, A. *et al.* (2016). A Study on Competency Mapping in Automobile Industry, *International Journal of Engineering Science and Computing, 6*(7), 8649-8657.

Shree, B, A. *et al.* (2016). A Study on Competency Mapping in Automobile Industry, *International Journal of Engineering Science and Computing, 6*(7), 8649-8657.

Singh, R. K., Garg, S. K., & Deshmukh, S. G. (2008). Competency and performance analysis of Indian SMEs and large organizations: An exploratory study. *Competitiveness Review: An International Business Journal, 18*(4), 308-321.

Sinha, D., Sinha, S., and Singh, K. (2016), Global HRM Review, Vol. 6, 86-94.

Skaalvik, E. M. (1997). Self-enhancing and self-defeating ego orientation: Relations with task and avoidance orientation, achievement, self-perceptions, and anxiety. *Journal of educational psychology, 89*(1), 71.

Solomon, D, M. (2013). Competency Mapping – A Holistic Approach for Industries. *PARIPEX - Indian Journal of Research, 2*(3).

Spencer, L. M., & Spencer, P. S. M. (2008). *Competence at Work models for superior performance*. John Wiley & Sons.

Spencer, L.M and Spencer, S.M. (1993). *Competence at Work*. New York: Wiley.

Stybel, L. J. (2010). Managing the inner contradictions of job descriptions: A technique for use in recruitment. *The Psychologist-Manager Journal, 13*(2), 105-110.

Tejaswari, A. and Ambuli, T.V. (2016).A Study on Competency Mapping of Employees with reference to Murugappan and Company. *International Journal of Research Science and Management, 3*(8), 21-31. https://ijrsm.com/index.php/journal-ijrsm/article/view/567

Thangasamy, E. (2014), Financial inclusion in North-East India: An analytical study, *International Journal of Commerce, Business and Management, 3*(1).

Tiwari (Mishra), S. (2012). Skills, Competencies And Employability Through Business Education. *AIMA Journal of Management & Research, 6*(4/4).

Turner, J.R. and Thayer, J. (2001). Introduction to Analysis of Variance. Design, Analysis and Interpretation. *Sage Publications, Inc.*

United Nations Industrial Development Organization. (2002). UNIDO Competencies. http://www.unido.org.

Velayudhan, M.T.K & Maran, K. (2009). A study on Mapping Core Competencies and development of Employees for Excellence with reference to HCL Technologies. *Journal of Contemporary Research in Management*, 53-67.

Waiker, V., Siddiqui, M. A. A., & Ansari, M. S. A. (2022). A Review Study On Employees' Competency Mapping And Output Management: With Reference Nagpur Based Small Scale Manufacturing Industries. *Journal of Positive School Psychology*, *6*(7), 4105-4111.

West, C. K., & Fish, J. A. (1973). *Relationship between self-concept and school achievement: A survey of empirical investigations* (Final rep.). Urbana, IL: National Institute of Education

White, R. (1959). Motivation reconsidered: The concept competence. *Psychological Review, 66*(5),279–333.

Worlikar, M. and Aggrawal, A. (2017). Review Study of Competency Mapping in the Organisations, *IOSR Journal of Business and Management,* 72-76.

Yuvaraj, R. (2011). Competency Mapping- A Drive for Indian Industries. *International Journal of Scientific and Engineering Research*, (8), 1-7.